DIG IN!

Earthdog Training Made Easy

Mario Migliorini

HOWELL
BOOK
HOUSE

New York

Howell Book House
A Simon and Schuster Macmillan Company
1633 Broadway
New York, NY 10019

MACMILLAN is a registered trademark of Macmillan, Inc.

Library of Congress Cataloging-in-Publication Data
Migliorini, Mario.
Dig in! earthdog training made easy / Mario Migliorini
    p. cm.
  Includes bibliographical references.
  1. Earthdog tests.   2. Terriers—Training.
  3. Dachshunds—Training.   4. Terriers   I. Title.
  SF425.53.M54   1997
  636.755—dc21   96-47580
                                            CIP
ISBN: 0-87605-568-4
Manufactured in the United States of America

99 98 97 9 8 7 6 5 4 3 2 1

Book Design: George McKeon
Cover Design: Kevin Hanek

CONTENTS

A Jack Russell Terrier going to ground in a natural earth. The fire of a determined earthdog burns with the same bright intensity above ground and below.

ABOUT THE AUTHOR

Mario Migliorini has trained and hunted with a wide variety of breeds ranging all the way from grade "A" racing and coursing Greyhounds to scruffy, nondescript hedge-hunting terriers.

The eldest son of an extremely proficient hunter, who was not averse to a little poaching on the side if necessary, Mario Migliorini started his apprenticeship in the field in England prior to the outbreak of World War II. Under the stern tutelage of his father, he learned to course hares and hedge-hunt for rabbits when he was barely eight years old.

A former dog trainer and professional handler on two continents, Mario and his wife Margaret have owned dogs of approximately forty different breeds, including many gun

The author with a young Lakeland Terrier.

The author and his father, pictured after a moderately productive day in the field, circa 1939.

dogs, working terriers and title-holders from all seven AKC Groups.

In 1959 Mario Migliorini exhibited the first Italian Spinoni, bred and shown in Great Britain, at the famed Crufts dog show.

A member of the Dog Writer's Association of America since 1969, Migliorini has written more than twenty-five books covering just about every aspect of dog care and training. His previous work for Howell Book House was the highly respected *Kennel Building and Management*, published in 1988.

As a former newspaper reporter and columnist, his articles have appeared in newspapers and most major American dog magazines starting with *Dog World* in 1961.

FOREWORD

I first met Mario Migliorini almost forty years ago, while we both were professional handlers, showing dogs primarily in the Midwest.

Mario was always meticulous—down to the last detail—and cared for the dogs he handled in the best way possible. He continually worked to be the best at his craft, and was always willing to help other exhibitors in any way he could.

I'm confident that this book will continue to further Mario Migliorini's thorough knowledge of training and handling dogs—this time in the new, exciting AKC Earthdog program.

Arley Hussin

Arley Hussin, a former professional handler and colleague of the author, is now a popular multiple Group judge officiating at more than seventy-five AKC-approved dog shows annually across the United States.

PREFACE

Much as modern rodeo events evolved to showcase the riding and livestock-handling ability of working cowboys, terrier sports were created to demonstrate the terriers' extraordinary ability to hunt and kill vermin in their many forms.

As one might expect, the always-resourceful terrier owners devised numerous ways of matching one dog's working ability against that of another for fun and profit. In addition to bragging rights, hefty side-bets and spectator wagering on the outcome of such matches made them all the more interesting.

In an era when, for the working classes of the British Isles, diversionary entertainment was virtually non-existent, dog sports become a national passion. It should be remembered, too, that during that period in history when brutal public executions were as popular and as well attended as the major sporting events of today, the concept of "inhumane" was still unknown.

My first purebred terrier was a West Highland White named Scottie. (Don't ask!) Scottie was perhaps two years old and amiable, but not what you would wholeheartedly call friendly. He was a dynamite hedge-hunter and a heck of a guard dog, but he was no one's pet.

His kennel was his castle; to encroach on his domain when he was in his residence was to risk painful consequences. We had several chickens running around the yard at the time, as most people did. My particular favorite was a small, speckled hen.

On one Sunday afternoon while the family was eating lunch, all hell broke loose outside. Chickens were cackling and squawking, and Scottie was barking vociferously at the top of his lungs. Maybe the ferrets were loose! Instead we found the speckled hen cackling loudly and strutting up and down in front of Scottie's kennel. The Westie, bristling with indignation, was standing his ground outside his kennel. He was glaring inside and barking and growling menacingly at the small oval object occupying his bed. It was the speckled hen's first egg.

From that day onward, whenever the speckled hen was ready to lay an egg, she would unceremoniously evict Scottie from his kennel, commandeer his bed and go to work. Immediately after the hen departed, the agitated terrier would go to the entrance to his kennel and bark in protest until the intruder was removed. Scottie the Terrible was afeared of an egg!

I first observed a working rat terrier in action at my father's Greyhound kennel. After a dozen derelict row-houses on a nearby lot were demolished, the abundant rodent population moved in with the neighbors. Rats invaded the shed where we kept our straw, creating all kinds of havoc.

When cats and a variety of traps proved totally ineffective, the local rat catcher was summoned to exterminate them. "Mr." Leathers—apparently a man without a given name—was a licensed vermin exterminator extraordinaire, so we were told. This was due to the fact that he was licensed by the National Department of Agriculture and was one of a handful of people authorized to use lethal poisons denied to the general public.

Leathers arrived in a shiny black car. He wore a dark, three-piece suit adorned with a large gold fob that dangled conspicuously across his middle. Apparently, it was his none-too-subtle way of elevating himself above the average working man. He was also accompanied by a trio of helpers:

Two teenage lads and a small, rough-and-ready Wire Fox Terrier.

Leathers conducted himself in a somewhat bombastic and supercilious manner. He was a living caricature of a man attempting to portray himself as someone of substance. Having made a niche for himself in the world, he revelled in his own view of his importance.

No "mornin'" or "what we got 'ere t'day?" from him. Instead, he sternly announced, "I'm Mr. Leathers. Where's your father, lad? Time is money, we don't have time to stand around here doing nothing all day, ya know!"

Quickly I summoned my father. When he arrived the two men engaged in a brief animated conversation, money changed hands and the ratting began.

"This place is made for rats," Leathers snorted, after a perfunctory look inside the wooden shed. He was correct, the building was packed from floor to ceiling with bales of fresh straw we used as bedding for a dozen or so racing Greyhounds.

"Hop to it!" Leathers snapped at his helpers. His teenage assistants opened the double doors, removed several bales to facilitate maneuverability, then began probing the straw with long bamboo poles.

The Fox Terrier had casually positioned himself six to eight feet outside the building, cutting off the angles much like a goalie does during a soccer or hockey match. The dog waited calmly—almost indifferent to the activity inside the building—until the first rat bolted into the open.

The instant the rat appeared the dog pounced. He grabbed the fleeing rodent and, with a single flick of the head, tossed it over his back. It landed several feet away, twitching in its final death throes. The dog paid the rat no mind; its spine was broken.

Then came a second rat, a third, a forth, a fifth—fifteen in all. A seemingly effortless killing machine, the little dog missed nary a one.

The trio worked with deft precision. They had developed a smooth, practiced cadence. The beaters methodically flushed the rats from the building in ones and twos, no more than the dog could handle.

When the rats stopped coming, Leathers, who claimed to be something of an alchemist, produced a small tin can filled with round bread pellets the size of peas, each laced with poison. Using an old teaspoon he conjured from his vest pocket, the ratter selectively distributed small amounts of his lethal bait at strategic locations.

"This is my own secret formula," he stated with pride. "Rats can't resist it. If there's any left inside the shed, this will take care of 'em. It never fails, I guarantee that!"

With that, Leathers and his crew departed, leaving behind the day's catch: fifteen Norwegian grey rats, some near half the size of an average cat. I was impressed. The year was 1945.

Today, ratters like Mr. Leathers are basically a vanished species, but we still have terriers much like those the ratter used to clear the shed. Happily, our dogs today still have the fire, determination and instinct to do the work that is the earthdog's heritage. However, while most small terriers and Dachshunds will never be called upon to enter an earth to battle with their traditional foes, many can do so with unrestrained enthusiasm if given the opportunity.

Now, with the implementation of AKC Earthdog Tests, we can test our dogs to see for ourselves that the proverbial spirit still glows warmly within them. That they can do this without risk of serious injury is an important plus. That we can enjoy their performance for ourselves and in the company of others who love these breeds, thrilling to their work, makes our pleasure truly complete.

It is my hope that *DIG IN! Earthdog Training Made Easy* helps you better prepare your dogs and yourself for the tests and that in being so prepared, you derive more pleasure from taking part.

EARTHDOG TESTS: THE BASICS

In brief, Earthdog Tests are standardized non-competitive meets, or digs, restricted to AKC registered Dachshunds and small terriers, breeds originally developed to go to ground in pursuit of vermin. The American Kennel Club's (AKC's) inaugural Earthdog Tests took place at a farm in Hillsboro, Oregon, from October 1-2, 1994. The two-day event was hosted by the Greater Portland Dachshund Club. The judges were William "Sil" Sanders and Karla Diethorn. (Similar tests have also been conducted under the auspices of the American Working Terrier Association (AWTA) and other interested organizations since the late 1960s and early 1970s.)

Emerging from a mixed entry of 155, mostly Dachshunds, came the first thirteen official AKC Junior Earthdog title holders in the United States. There were nine Dachshunds, two Border Terriers, a Scottie and a Cairn. It was an auspicious start to a new, exciting discipline.

WHAT ARE EARTHDOG TESTS?

Earthdog Tests are a way of assessing a den dog's natural or trained hunting and working ability under relatively safe, simulated hunting conditions, utilizing a man-made underground lair. The tests are comprised of an introductory phase, called the Introduction to Quarry (or Intro), and three noncompetitive trials, each of which is progressively more difficult.

The first thirteen recipients of AKC Junior Earthdog (JE) titles awarded at the inaugural AKC Earthdog Tests. Judge Kala Diethorn is shown at the extreme left in the back row.

Participants "pass" or "fail" according to the trial judge's assessment of each dog's performance that day. (The criteria by which a judge's decision is made are outlined in Chapter 2, "AKC Earthdog Test Rules.") As with all subjective procedures, individual interpretation of the rules many vary from one official to another. This makes it important that handlers understand and comply with the judges' instructions. Errors made by the handler result in penalties for the dog. Owners and handlers are governed by the AKC's rules of good conduct and sportsmanship; histrionics inside or outside the official test area have no place at an Earthdog Trial.

Introduction to Quarry is the first Earthdog Test and is something like a schooling (or practice) run. The dog does not receive any qualifications or titles. It is composed of abbreviated den work intended to acquaint the novice dog with the two most basic procedures: entering a hole and barking at rodents.

A portion of a typical Earthdog Test liner, showing two 90 degree turns, that has been installed above ground for exhibition purposes. For qualifying trials, similar den liners are buried approximately twelve inches into the ground, then covered with soil and natural debris to simulate a natural earth. Were this an actual qualifying event, the only sections of the liner visible to spectators would be the entrance and exit(s). Earthdog clubs frequently use unburied den liners for training and practice sessions.

Burying a den liner in preparation for an AKC Earthdog event.

Customarily held in conjunction with the other Earthdog title tests, the Intro is not so much a bona fide test as it is a first encounter of two designated adversaries: the dog and the rat. For prospective Earthdogs, Introduction to Quarry is the first rite of passage and possibly an indication of their gameness and enthusiasm for what lies ahead. It provides young and/or inexperienced den dogs with the opportunity to demonstrate their willingness to access and explore an unfamiliar earth and confront the occupants; namely, a pair of caged rats.

Because a dog's first outing may be marred by any number of variables, owners should not regard a poor performance as either a failure or a waste of time. Training can right many wrongs.

After the IQ test, dogs advance through the ranks by gradual progression. Certificates of accomplishment are awarded at each of three levels: Junior Earthdog (JE), Senior Earthdog (SE), and Master Earthdog (ME). Each test requires a greater degree of desire, gameness and den savvy than the previous one. Added intensity and determination are needed in pursuing game to ground and finding and working the quarry under increasingly more difficult den conditions.

Finally, it is important to emphasize that dogs remain under the handler's control at all times. The need for adequate control is emphasized by the recall from the den exercise, specifically required in the SE trials as explained in Phase Two. Please keep in mind, Earthdog Tests should be regarded as a sport or pastime, nothing more, nothing less.

Phase One: Introduction to Quarry (Intro)

Introduction to the quarry is a relatively painless schooling run designed to encourage neophyte Earthdogs to go to ground and confront an unknown quarry waiting in a cage at the opposite end of a short chute or tunnel. Hopefully, Intro will provide dogs with a positive experience, boost their

Introduction to Quarry is the name of the first level in developing a competitive Earthdog. This Longhaired Dachshund appears somewhat hesitant at the prospect of meeting the unknown.

adrenaline, and fire up previously dormant vermin-killing instincts supposedly acquired from past generations of working ancestors. In reality, a great deal more depends on one's training and handling of his or her dog than on the unknown predisposition of its long departed kin.

Not a prerequisite for participation in titled tests, Intro is more of a **taste** than a test; a teaser, one might say. The only reward is a positive experience that should help a dog's psyche and mental preparedness for future tests. To the owner it provides a rough guide to the type of training the dog may need.

The introduction requires a dog to enter and negotiate a ten-foot liner with a single entrance and one 90 degree turn. To pass this test a dog must enter the den and locate the caged rats in under two minutes from the time he's released and work them for an additional thirty seconds. "Work" means actively attempting to reach or intimidate the quarry by digging, barking, growling, clawing, scratching, lunging, or

5

The owner of an Earthdog prospect waits in anticipation as, watched by interested spectators, the den master coaxes a reluctant trainee toward the quarry. To pass the Intro a dog must reach the quarry, unaided, within two minutes or less from the time he is released ten feet from the den opening.

"Hello!" A totally engrossed Lakeland Terrier meets the blasé quarry. The unconcerned rat is completely protected in its wire cage.

A Border terrier "working the quarry," appears unaware that the overhead trapdoor has been opened.

biting. Standing motionless at the end of the tunnel, giving the rats the *evil eye*, does not constitute "working."

The test starts within the designated test area, with the handler holding his or her dog no higher than waist level. At the judge's signal, he or she must release the dog at least ten feet from the tunnel entrance. Deliberately launching the dog in the direction of the den entrance is definitely not permitted.

Having been released, a dog has two minutes to locate and enter the den, then it must find the quarry and work it continuously for an additional thirty seconds. A handler is permitted to give only one command. Any additional sound, movement, or gesture could be construed by the judge as a second command.

Having released the dog, a handler should remain silent and motionless and await the judge's signal. However, should a dog seem nervous, hesitant or disoriented by its strange surroundings, the handler may approach the liner and stand quietly beside the entrance to the den and wait.

This sounds easy enough. And it is, provided the dog knows what to do, instinctively or from previous training. The latter is by far the more reliable option.

If a dog is reluctant to work after reaching the quarry, the judge may encourage him verbally or by shaking the rat cage.

After the dog has successfully worked the quarry, the judge will signal the handler to remove him from the tunnel through the overhead trapdoor in the liner, marking an end to the Intro.

Phase Two: Junior Earthdog (JE)

The Junior Earthdog Test (JE) is the first of three tests by which Dachshunds and the following working terrier breeds can acquire AKC Junior Earthdog titles:

Australian Terrier
Bedlington Terrier
Border Terrier
Cairn Terrier
Dandie Dinmont Terrier
Fox Terrier (Smooth and Wire)
Lakeland Terrier
Norfolk Terrier
Norwich Terrier
Scottish Terrier
Sealyham Terrier
Skye Terrier
Welsh Terrier
West Highland White Terrier

Dogs that are disfigured or have been scarred by accident or injury may participate unless physically handicapped to the point where they cannot function normally. Deaf or blind dogs are not eligible, period. Two qualifying scores from two different judges will gain a dog its Junior Earthdog title (JE after its name) and make him eligible to move up to Senior Earthdog trials.

Whether liners are placed above or below ground, Intro and JE dogs are removed from the tunnel through a small trapdoor conveniently located, near the quarry, at the end of the liner.

Participants at Senior Earthdog Tests are required to enter the den via a vertical instead of horizontal opening in the liner. They are also required to leave the den when recalled by the handler, after the quarry has "bolted." This, however, is an unlikely response for dogs not adequately prepared in advance.

The JE test liner must measure a minimum of thirty feet long with three 90 degree turns. The entrance should be clearly visible, allowing both dog and handler to see inside, and made to look as inviting as possible.

The release is identical to the Intro: waist high, ten feet from the hole. The time allowed for JE dogs to reach the quarry is thirty seconds. Having reached the quarry, a dog is allowed an additional thirty seconds to start working. Once the dog starts, he must work unabated for one full minute within a foot of the quarry.

At the conclusion of the JE Test, the handler retrieves his or her charge as described for the Intro.

Phase Three: Senior Earthdog (SE)

The Senior Earthdog Test is divided into three parts: locating the quarry, working the quarry, and leaving the den when called by the handler.

The release point is moved back an additional ten feet from the entrance to the earth, and the distance from the drop point to the liner is marked with the quarry's scent.

The entrance to the den is converted from horizontal to vertical by building a mound of packed dirt around it, to make it appear somewhat less inviting. Following the suggestions made later in the book makes the change to the entrance inconsequential insofar as den work is concerned.

Although still basically thirty feet long with three right-angle turns, the SE test tunnel has two added features: a false den and a false exit. The false den is four feet long with no exit; however, it does contain scented bedding material to simulate a recently vacated nest area. The false exit is seven feet long with one 90 degree turn.

The time allowed to reach the quarry is ninety seconds. To qualify, a dog must run the entire thirty feet of the tunnel proper. He may exit, but not enter, via the false den opening, which remains unscented at all times.

The unscented den is actually something of a fallacy. The first dog to enter the false den contaminates the ground with the scent on its feet. As other dogs follow, the scent grows even stronger.

Upon reaching the quarry, a dog has fifteen seconds to begin working. After ninety seconds of uninterrupted work, the judge removes the rat cage from the hole and signals the handler to recall the dog. (Removing the rats from the earth signifies the quarry has bolted, or left the den.)

At the judge's signal, a handler may call or whistle to his or her charge. Using bait, squeakers, toys, rattles and bells to lure or entice a dog out of the hole is unacceptable. A dog then has ninety seconds to comply and is not penalized for leaving from the false exit. A handler may call his or her dog as often as needed within the allotted time and, if able to do so, may reach in and pull the dog out of the hole.

After being recalled from the den and following the removal of the quarry, a dog must return to its handler, who must have control of him within ninety seconds. Experienced handlers have even been known to concentrate so hard on hollering down one hole that he or she failed to see the dog emerge from another.

In most cases, dogs are unlikely to perform the recall exercise without prior training. This is because untrained, highly adrenalized dogs are predisposed to temporary deafness.

To obtain a Senior Earthdog title, a dog must pass a total of three qualifying runs. Also, there must be a different judge for at least one of these runs.

A dog with an SE title may continue to enter SE tests or graduate to Master Earthdog tests. In most cases, owners would probably choose to move up the ladder. However, the initial shortage of ME entries and suitable venues in certain areas of the country may necessitate continued participation in SE tests as a way to keep one's dog sharp and at the top of its game.

Phase Four: Master Earthdog (ME)

Because Master Earthdog tests require dogs to work in pairs, the test was initially viewed with skepticism, possibly more so by owners of terriers than of Dachshunds. Objections were voiced over certain aspects of the test that required participating dogs to act in a manner that some owners considered contrary to "normal" terrier behavior. Owners were worried that overly aggressive dogs might attack, intimidate, or seriously injure a smaller bracemate—a serious concern for owners of show dogs.

So far fewer problems have occurred under actual trial conditions than were first anticipated. Even so, ME is a somewhat elite test and not well-suited to every dog. In all candor, this is as it should be.

The ME is a test unlike those previously described, inasmuch as participants are required to work in pairs—unfamiliar bracemates matched together by the luck of the draw. In this test, the importance of training and owner control is vastly more important than at the lower levels. The test is composed of four parts, as indicated in the rules in Chapter 2.

Each brace is released 100 yards from the entrance to the den. The first dog to reach the hole runs first; the other has to watch or "honor" its bracemate. A time-honored practice with pointing dogs, "honoring" a bracemate would be a doubtful occurrence in the field where hard-charging terriers are concerned, but no matter.

Consider the den as point "A" and the location of the drop area as point "B." A scent line is laid down for approximately twenty feet from point A, in the general direction of point B.

To test the dogs' savvy and serve as a diversion, a clearly visible but unscented entrance to a false den is located midway between points A and B, but several feet away from the scent line. This provides a clear advantage to dogs that rely on their noses more than on their eyes. Dogs may investigate, but not work, the false den; e.g., start barking. To do so is to fail.

The judge first stands with the handlers at the starting line. As they release their dogs, he or she starts walking towards the hole. The dogs must reach the hole ahead of the official—in about one minute. Failing to do so means failing the test.

To pass this leg of the test, dogs are required to locate the real entrance. In addition to the fact that the "real" entrance is not readily visible, it is also temporarily plugged with a removable stopper. A judge's steward is also stationed near the blocked entrance to control inappropriate canine interaction, an interesting assignment for anyone. And within the den liner, a constriction area and an obstacle have been added. (See Chapter 2, "Den Specifications, Section 14" for further information.) Failure to locate or show interest in the real entrance means failing the test, but testing may continue anyway.

If necessary, the handler of the first dog to reach and indicate the tunnel will remove his or her dog so as not to impede or help its bracemate from also finding the den. While the first dog to the hole is being tested, the "honoring" bracemate is collared and staked out on a short chain, approximately ten feet from the hole. Handlers of honoring dogs will remain with them and may caution them to be quiet, which is not always easy to do when dogs are highly excited. According to AKC rules: "The dog must show interest, and may occasionally be vocal, but shall not bark continuously."[1]

The den test requires the participating dog to locate the quarry within ninety seconds or less, then work it for an additional ninety seconds.

While the dog is working the quarry, the judge will attempt to distract him by tapping and scratching the top of the liner for thirty seconds (using a stick or similar object) to simulate digging noises that the dog inside the liner must ignore. During this part of the test, the judge and handler of the dog in the hole remain together.

At the conclusion of the test, the first dog is picked up and assumes the honoring role for its bracemate. The second dog is allowed to run the same as the first.

To qualify, a dog must pass each part of the test. Tests are likely to be modified in time, in order to keep up with changing requirements.

To earn its ME title, a dog must qualify at four separate digs (or meets) under two different judges.

The doubts some owners express concerning facets of the ME test are valid and completely understandable. However, the tests that precede this highest level of participation should effectively purge the trials of overly aggressive or disruptive dogs and those whose performance is of questionable merit. The rules state: "If in the judge's opinion a dog's performance was prejudiced by peculiar or unusual conditions it may be retested immediately or later in the day . . . "[2]

Finally, regardless of whether or not a dog is seriously injured or intimidated from an attack by another dog, it is more than likely to affect the victim's performance, temporarily or even permanently. Therefore, there is obvious merit to the suggestion that dogs exhibiting consistently unacceptable behavior should be permanently banned from entering den trials. Whether or not that becomes necessary, time alone will tell.

1 AKC Rules are reproduced with the permission of the American Kennel Club.
2 Ibid.

AKC EARTHDOG TEST RULES

CHAPTER 1

Section 1. Purpose. The purpose of non-competitive Earthdog tests is to offer breeders and owners of small Terriers and Dachshunds a standardized gauge to measure their dogs' natural and trained hunting and working abilities when exposed to a hunting situation. The noncompetitive program begins with a basic introduction to den work and quarry and progresses through gradual steps to require the dog to demonstrate that it is capable of being trained to follow game to ground and work its quarry.

Earthdog tests are a sport and all participants should be guided by the principles of good sportsmanship both in and outside the test field.

Section 2. Earthdog Tests Defined. A member earthdog test is a test at which qualifications for titles are awarded, given by a club or association which is a member of The American Kennel Club.

A licensed earthdog test is a test at which qualifications for titles are awarded, given by a club or association which is not a member of the American Kennel Club, but which has been licensed by the American Kennel Club to hold the test.

Sanctioned earthdog tests are informal events at which dogs may participate but not for titles, held by a club or association by obtaining the sanction of the American Kennel Club.

Generally, sanctioned events are held by clubs to qualify for approval to hold licensed or member club events.

Section 3. AKC Rules Applying to Registration and Discipline. All of AKC's Rules applying to Registration and Discipline shall apply to all Earthdog tests held under these Regulations.

Section 4. Eligibility of Dogs. Dogs six months of age or older and registered with the American Kennel Club are eligible to participate in Earthdog tests, as are spayed and neutered dogs and dogs with Limited Registration provided they are classified as eligible breeds.

Dogs of an eligible breed that have been granted Indefinite Listing Privileges (ILP) are eligible to participate. A dog of an eligible breed with an acceptable foreign registration number is eligible to participate subject to Chapter 11, Section 1 of the Dog Show Rules.

The following breeds are classified as eligible to participate in Earthdog tests: Dachshunds, Australian Terriers, Bedlington Terriers, Border Terriers, Cairn Terriers, Dandie Dinmont Terriers, Fox Terriers (Smooth and Wire), Lakeland Terriers, Norfolk Terriers, Norwich Terriers, Scottish Terriers, Sealyham Terriers, Skye Terriers, Welsh Terriers and West Highland White Terriers.

Inasmuch as Dachshunds and Terriers are hunting dogs, dogs disfigured as the result of accident or injury but otherwise qualified shall be eligible provided that the disfigurement does not interfere with functional movement. Dogs that are blind and deaf shall not be eligible. Blind means without useful vision, and deaf means without useful hearing.

A dog is not eligible to enter a test if the Judge of that test or any member of that Judge's family owns or co-owns the dog. The word "family" shall include a spouse, a sibling, a parent or a child, whether natural or adopted, of the Judge in question but shall not extend to other blood or legal relations.

Bitches in season shall not be eligible to enter the test. Entry fees paid for a bitch that comes into season shall not be refunded.

Section 5. Eligibility to Hold Earthdog Tests. The Board of Directors of the American Kennel Club may, at its discretion, grant permission to clubs or associations to hold Earthdog tests which shall be governed by such Rules and Regulations as from time to time shall be determined by the Board of Directors.

Section 6. Making Application. A club or association that meets the requirements of the American Kennel Club that wishes to hold an Earthdog test at which qualifications for titles may be earned must make application to the American Kennel Club on the form provided for permission to hold the event. An application fee of $35.00 must accompany each application. If the club or association fails to hold its event at the approved time and place, the amount of the application fee shall be returned.

Applications for licensed or member earthdog tests must be received by the American Kennel Club at least 90 days prior to the date(s) of the event.

A club may be approved to hold up to four licensed or member events in a calendar year. A club can be approved to hold two events on one weekend provided the same Judges do not judge the same tests.

A club or association that meets all of the requirements of the American Kennel Club may be approved to hold a sanctioned test by applying on a form provided by the American Kennel Club and paying an application fee of $15.00. Applications for sanctioned tests must be filed with the AKC at least four weeks prior to the date(s) of the event.

All of these Regulations shall govern sanctioned tests except for those which specifically state that they apply to licensed and member tests.

Section 7. Earthdog Test Secretary and Earthdog Test Chairman. A club holding an Earthdog test must name a Test Secretary and Test Chairman. The Chairman must be a member of the club. The premium list for all licensed or member tests shall designate the Test Secretary as receiving entries. Test Secretaries and Chairmen shall be ineligible to Judge at the event in which they act in these official capacities.

Section 8. Appointment of Earthdog Test Committee. A club or association that has been granted permission by the American Kennel Club to hold a test must appoint an Earthdog Test Committee which will have complete responsibility for planning and conducting the event. This committee shall be comprised of at least five club members (including the Chairman) and shall ensure the safe, efficient, and orderly conduct of the event. The Committee must have on hand, on the day of the test, assistance and materials sufficient to efficiently make repairs to the test area and must ensure that the area is free of dangerous materials or conditions.

The Committee is responsible for compliance with all of these Regulations except those which come under the sole jurisdiction of the Judges.

Section 9. Veterinarian. Every club holding a licensed or member test shall arrange to have a veterinarian in attendance throughout the duration of the test. The club may elect to have a veterinarian "on call" but must ensure that veterinary assistance will be available should it be needed. The premium list must state whether the veterinarian will be in attendance or "on call."

Section 10. Declining Entries. A Test Committee may decline any entries or may remove any dog from the event for cause, but in each such instance shall file good and sufficient reasons for doing so with the American Kennel Club.

Section 11. Ribbons and Rosettes. A club or association holding a licensed or member test shall offer a ribbon or rosette to each dog that qualifies.

Each ribbon or rosette shall be at least two inches wide and approximately eight inches long, and shall bear on the face a facsimile of the seal of the American Kennel Club, the words "Earthdog Test" and "qualifying," and the name of the test-giving club or association. Ribbons and rosettes shall be dark green in color, and rosettes shall have a white center streamer and white button. Additional required information (name of class, date, and location of the event) may be printed on the ribbon or rosette, or may be affixed on the back with labels. If ribbons or rosettes are awarded at sanctioned tests, they shall be light green.

Section 12. Risk. Owners or handlers entering dogs in a test do so at their own risk and agree to assume responsibility for any damage caused by them or by their dogs. They also agree to abide by all of the Rules and Regulations of the American Kennel Club.

Section 13. Premium Lists. A premium list be must be provided for licensed or member club tests.

The premium list shall be printed (any printing or copying process is acceptable), and shall state whether the event is "licensed by the American Kennel Club" or held by an "AKC Member club." Premium lists shall measure not less than $5^{1}/_{2} \times 8^{1}/_{2}$ inches nor more than $8^{1}/_{2} \times 11$ inches.

The following information shall be included in the premium list for a licensed or member test: Name of the club or association offering the test, the exact location and date of the test, name and address of the Test Chairman, names of the Test Committee members (minimum of five including Chairman), time testing shall commence, entry fees, tests offered, names and addresses of Judges including their assignments; name, address, and phone number of the Test Secretary, date and closing time of entries, a listing of the club officers with addresses, and an official AKC entry form. Premium lists shall also include the name and address of the veterinarian(s) on duty or on call during the test, and specify whether ribbons or rosettes will be offered.

At least four copies of the premium list must be mailed to AKC at the time of mailing to prospective entrants.

Section 14. Closing of Entries, Running Order. The closing time for entries, and the location at which entries shall be taken shall be printed in the premium list. Entries for a licensed or member club test may close at any time prior to the start of each test level.

If entries are to be limited, the numerical limitation(s) must be stated in the premium list and entries will close when the numerical limit or limits have been reached.

A club or association holding a licensed or member club test shall not accept any entries received after the closing date and time specified on the premium list.

At the option of the test-giving club, dogs may be run in the order that entries are received or the running order may be established by a random drawing of entries in each class. In either case, multiple entries from the same handler should be separated when possible. The Test Committee or the Judges may modify the running order to expedite the running of the test. Each entry in a licensed or member club test must be made on an official American Kennel Club entry form. Each entry form must be completed in full and must be signed by the owner or his agent duly authorized to make the entry, and the information given on the form must be that which applies to the entered dog.

Section 15. Recording Fees. At every licensed or member test held under these Regulations, a recording fee of $3.00 shall be required for each entry.

The recording fee is to help defray expenses involved in maintaining the records and applies to all entries, regardless of whether they participate.

Section 16. Submission of Records. Clubs holding licensed or member club tests must utilize the standard AKC official judges report sheets which will be automatically supplied to the Test Secretary following approval of the judging panel.

Within seven days of the completion of a licensed or member club test, the Test Secretary shall forward to the American Kennel Club the official judges report sheets containing the names and other identifying information for all qualified dogs. The judges sheets must be signed and certified by the judge(s) and the Test Secretary, and forwarded to the AKC with all entry forms, a complete Test Secretary's report, and the recording fees.

A club or association holding a licensed or member club test shall retain a copy of the official judges' sheets for at least one year.

Section 17. Cancellation of Awards. If an ineligible dog has been entered and run in a licensed or member club test, or if the person or persons named as owner or owners on the entry form are not the person or persons who actually owned the dog at the time entries closed, or if the dog is run in a class for which it is not entered, or if its entry form is deemed invalid by the American Kennel Club under the Rules and Regulations, all resulting awards shall be canceled by the American Kennel Club.

If an award is canceled by the American Kennel Club, the entrant of the dog shall return all prizes to the Secretary of the test-giving club within 10 days of receipt of notice from the American Kennel Club of said cancellation.

Section 18. Disturbances. Barking dogs outside the test area are to be removed from the area but should not be disciplined for barking.

The Judge must promptly remove from participation any dog which cannot be controlled, and may excuse any dog he or she considers unfit to participate.

The Judge must also promptly remove any handler who willfully interferes with another dog or handler, or who abuses his or her dog in the test area, or in any way displays conduct prejudicial to the sport of pure-bred dogs and the American Kennel Club, and must report such incidents to the Test Committee for further action under Chapter 5 of AKC's Registration and Discipline Rules. (Refer also to AKC's Guide for Event Committees in Handling Misconduct which is supplied to the Test Secretary.)

CHAPTER 2

Instructions for Test Committees and Judges

Section 1. Approval of Judges. Judges officiating at licensed or member club tests must be approved by the American Kennel Club. A club or association may submit the name of any approved Judges for approval to have the Judge officiate at the test. Such approved Judges may enter dogs in any classes which they are not judging, and for which they are not advertised as Judges.

Section 2. Judges Decisions, Responsibilities. The decisions of the Judge shall be final in all matters relating to the performance of the dog. Full discretionary power is given to the Judge to withhold any and all qualifications for want of merit.

The Judge is responsible for making the test meaningful and challenging, but never out of reach of the dog and handler who, at an Introduction to Quarry test may never have been presented with an open earth before. The Judge's function is to educate as well as evaluate.

The Judge is responsible for ensuring compliance with these Regulations throughout a test, and for ensuring that the quarry is properly cared for during the event.

Section 3. Judges and Test Committee's Responsibilities. The Test Committee and officials of the club holding the test are responsible for providing the quarry, den liners, test material, facilities and equipment which meet the requirements of the Regulations.

The Judge must check the quarry, test layout, and den liners before starting the test. The Judge shall also supervise the scenting and covering of the dens before starting the test. If the Judge deems the facilities, test layout, or den construction inadequate for the event and no corrections or modifications can be made, the Judge shall cancel the event. Entry fees shall be refunded by the Test Committee, and the Judge reimbursed for his or her expenses. The Judge shall not receive any additional fees that might have previously been agreed upon.

The Test Committee and the Judge shall have the option of rescheduling the event, and, if rescheduled, refunds shall be made only to those handlers that decline to participate in the rescheduled test.

Section 4. Judge's Stewards and Apprentices. Each Judge shall have assigned to him or her a Judge's Steward. Test Stewards should also be appointed to assist in the conduct of the event and in control of the test area. At the Judge's discretion, an apprentice Judge may be in the test area, and may score the dogs independently but the apprentice Judge's scores shall not be considered in determining whether a dog passes or fails. They may listen as the Judge explains the results of the test to the participants, but may not offer any additional comments to the participants. Only one apprentice Judge may be permitted in the test area at one time. An apprentice Judge may serve as the Judge's Steward. Apprentice Judges' score sheets shall not be distributed to participants and must be filed with the Test Secretary at the conclusion of the test for forwarding to the American Kennel Club.

Section 5. Retesting. If, in the Judge's opinion, a dog's performance was prejudiced by peculiar and unusual conditions, the dog may be retested either immediately or later in the day at the discretion of the Judge.

Section 6. Scoring, Announcements of Score. The tests shall be scored on a pass (qualifying) or fail (non-qualifying) basis in accord with the qualifying performance descriptions in Chapter 4 of these Regulations.

The names of the dogs that have qualified shall be posted promptly for public viewing either during the test or after the completion of each test. The Test Secretary or Judge will present ribbons to the dogs which have qualified at the completion of each test.

CHAPTER 3

Classes, Qualifying Scores, Awarding of Titles

Section 1. Classes. The classes at a licensed or member test are Introduction to Quarry (non-regular with no credit toward titles), Junior Earthdog, Senior Earthdog and Master Earthdog. Clubs may offer any or all classes at licensed and member club events. All classes are open to all eligible dogs (see Chapter 1, Section 4) except as specified in Sections 4 and 5 of this Chapter.

Classes are run in the order determined by the Test Committee, but the Master Earthdog Test should be run before the other classes.

Section 2. Qualifying Scores. The total number of qualifications required for the issuance of the titles Junior Earthdog, Senior Earthdog and Master Earthdog shall be established by the Board of Directors of the American Kennel Club.

Section 3. Junior Earthdog Class and Title (JE). The Junior Earthdog class is open to all eligible dogs (see Chapter 1, Section 4).

In order to be recorded as a Junior Earthdog, a dog must be registered in the AKC Stud Book, and must have a record of having qualified in the Junior Earthdog test in two (2) AKC licensed or member club tests under two different Judges.

Upon completion of these requirements, an AKC Junior Earthdog (JE) certificate will be issued to the owner, and the dog shall be identified as a Junior Earthdog in all official AKC records by the suffix title JE. A dog that has been recorded as a Junior Earthdog may continue to enter the Junior Earthdog test, but no further Junior Earthdog certificates will be issued.

Section 4. Senior Earthdog Class and Title (SE). The Senior Earthdog class is open only to dogs that have acquired the Junior Earthdog title. (Prior to October 1, 1995, dogs with equivalent titles from another organization may enter this class without a JE title.)

In order to be recorded as a Senior Earthdog, a dog must be registered in the AKC Stud Book, and must have a record of having qualified in the Senior Earthdog test at three (3) AKC licensed or member club tests under two different Judges.

Upon completion of these requirements, an AKC Senior Earthdog (SE) certificate will be issued to the owner, and the dog shall be identified as a Senior Earthdog in all official AKC records by the suffix title SE, which shall supersede the JE title. A dog that has been recorded as a Senior Earthdog may continue to enter the Senior Earthdog test, but no further Senior Earthdog certificates will be issued. Dogs that have qualified in a Senior Earthdog test at an AKC licensed or member test are ineligible to enter Junior Earthdog tests.

Section 5. Master Earthdog Class and Title (ME). The Master Earthdog class is open only to dogs that have acquired the Senior Earthdog title.

In order to be recorded as a Master Earthdog, a dog must be registered in the AKC Stud Book, and must have a record of having qualified in the Master Earthdog test at four (4) AKC licensed or member club hunting tests under two different Judges.

Upon completion of these requirements, an AKC Master Earthdog (ME) certificate will be issued to the owner and the dog will be identified as a Master Earthdog in all official AKC records by the suffix title ME which shall supersede any AKC earthdog test title that may have been previously earned.

A dog that has been recorded as a Master Earthdog may continue to enter the Master Earthdog test but no further Master Earthdog certificates will be issued.

Dogs that have qualified in a Master Earthdog test at an AKC licensed or member club test are ineligible to enter Junior and Senior Earthdog tests.

CHAPTER 4

Den Specifications, Running and Judging, Test and Performance Descriptions

Section 1. Test Area Conditions and Dimensions. The test area for the Introduction to Quarry test shall be no less than 40 feet by 40 feet, with no portion of the den including the point of release, less than 10 feet from the side of the test area.

The test area(s) for the Junior, Senior and Master tests shall be of a size sufficient to contain the den, with no portion of the den including the point of release less than 20 feet from the edge of the test area.

Clubs should use a barrier or otherwise demarcate a test area to prevent spectator interference with the work of the dogs. The earth shall be prepared to look as natural as possible. Brush and other natural material may be used to prepare the earth but should not block the entrance to the earth. The entrance should look as inviting to the dog as possible. The test area for all tests shall be clearly marked, shall not contain unsafe conditions, and shall be free of dangerous materials.

The liners for the dens shall be constructed to ensure a safe and danger-free environment for dogs, quarry, handlers and Judges. The basic den construction allows for a tunnel approximately nine (9) inches by nine (9) inches, which is large enough for all dogs in the eligible breeds.

The liners shall be set in the ground such that when the liners are covered the top surface of the liner is not visible. The liners must be well covered, and the top of the liner (not visible) must be flush with the ground. Care shall be taken to assure that the bottom surface of the earth is reasonably smooth and as even as possible.

The dens shall be located so as to minimize outside distractions. The earth may be dug the day before the trial, but no dog shall be allowed to enter the earth before judging begins. The Judge shall oversee the placement of the liners and the scenting of the den on the day of the test. Only the dog currently being tested shall be allowed in the test area. Under no circumstances shall more than one dog be allowed in the test area at any time. Spectators shall be allowed outside the test area provided that they are quiet, and do not distract the dogs. No dogs shall be allowed in the area immediately adjacent to the test area. The dogs waiting to be tested shall be kept at least 100 feet from the perimeter of the test area, in a holding area so designated.

The dens shall be scented, using a specified scent, to simulate an actual den. In the Introduction to Quarry and Junior Earthdog tests, the entire length of the den must be scented, no more than one hour before the start of the test. In the Senior and Master Earthdog tests, the scent line shall be laid only on the primary quarry trial. Extreme care must be taken not to allow false trails to receive any scent which may unnecessarily confuse the dogs. The Judge shall be responsible for overseeing the correct scenting of the dens.

The scent trail shall be laid evenly from a point under the quarry cage to a point two feet past the entrance of the den. If, in the opinion of the Judge, the scent trail has weakened due to the number of dogs entering the earth, the Judge shall direct the Test Steward or Judge's Steward to lightly rescent the den, using a spray bottle or scent drag. Care should be taken by those actually scenting the earth to lay the scent trail in a manner consistent with real life conditions.

Section 2. Quarry Requirements and Care. The quarry to be used shall be two adult rats. Two rats are required and shall be securely caged at all times. Water and food must be provided for the rats during the trial. The Judge shall be responsible for the care and safety of the quarry during the test.

Alternatively, clubs can use an artificial quarry which should be located behind a barrier, properly scented and capable of movement (i.e. simulated lunging). For example, an ice fishing jig set sideways to hit the front of the cage would be acceptable.

The quarry will be placed in the den just before the beginning of the test. The den will then be securely covered to prevent the dog from scenting the quarry from above.

Section 3. Qualifying Performances. The Judge's certification of a qualifying performance for any dog constitutes certification to the American Kennel Club that the dog on this occasion has evidenced abilities at least in accordance with minimum standards and that the abilities demonstrated justify the awarding of the title for the class. A qualifying score must never be awarded to a dog which has not exhibited abilities that meet the minimum requirements.

Section 4. Introduction to Quarry. This test is a simple instinct test requiring no training or previous exposure to earthwork. No titles are earned and it is not a prerequisite for advanced tests. Young dogs, dogs with no previous working experience, and novice handlers are encouraged to enter. Inasmuch as it may be the first den experience for some dogs, the Judge and the handler shall do their utmost to assure that it is a positive experience for the dog.

The Judge shall be allowed to use discretion in encouraging the dog by scratching or moving the cage, or some other method felt necessary to get a true reaction from the dog.

The dog shall be brought to the test area entrance on a lead. The Test Steward shall instruct the handler to remove the collar and lead, and the handler shall carry the dog to the starting marker. The handler may encourage the dog up to this point. The Judge must make sure that each handler understands the test requirements before starting the dog.

Section 5. Introductory Test—Den Design. The den for the test shall be the standard liners approximately nine (9) inches by nine (9) inches, set so as to provide a tunnel approximately 10 feet in length, with one 90 degree turn. The handler shall release the dog from a point directly in front of the den, approximately 10 feet from the entrance. The Judge and Steward shall attempt to provide as little distraction as possible.

Section 6. Introductory Test—Qualifying Performance. The Judge shall direct the handler to give the dog one command to release the dog. The handler shall release the dog from a point no higher than waist level. Placing the dog on the ground before release is permitted. Throwing the dog in the direction of the den entrance shall not be permitted, and shall cause the dog to fail. The handler may give one short command, but shall remain silent with no further command or signal until instructed otherwise by the Judge. Further encouragement may cause the dog to fail. The handler may walk to the den entrance and quietly stand at the den entrance. The Judge or the Judge's Steward shall time the test. The time shall start when the dog enters the earth. The dog shall be allowed two minutes from the time it first enters the earth to begin working the quarry. The dog may exit and re-enter the earth during the time allowed, provided it has not started working the quarry. (Note: In all tests the quarry is in a protective cage and cannot come into contact with the dog.)

The dog shall not qualify if it requires over two minutes to reach the quarry. Once the dog begins working the quarry, the Judge or Judge's Steward shall begin timing the working time, and shall continue timing until the dog quits or the time limit is reached. Once the dog begins working it must work continuously for 30 seconds, with no encouragement, to qualify. Work is defined as digging, barking, growling, lunging, biting at the quarry, or any other action which, in the opinion of the Judge, indicates the dog's interest in the quarry. Any definite break in the dog's work shall stop the time, but a change from one form of work to another shall not stop the time as long as the dog continues working in a natural manner.

If, in the Judge's opinion, the dog is not reacting to the presence of the quarry, the Judge may attempt to interest the dog with no penalty to the dog. This may include shaking the quarry cage, tapping or scratching the cage, or use of a noisemaker, but should cease as soon as the dog begins working. Since the test is designed for dogs with little or no experience, mild encouragement by the Judge shall not cause a failure.

Dogs which reach the quarry within two minutes and work continuously for 30 seconds, shall pass.

At the completion of the test, the Judge shall announce the names of dogs that passed. The test-giving club may award prizes or trophies to the dogs passing.

Section 7. Junior Earthdog Test. The evaluation of a dog's ability can never be precise. However the primary purpose of the small Terriers and Dachshunds is to pursue quarry to ground, hold the game, and alert the hunter where to dig, or to bolt. Whether the dog is successful in its primary purpose is determined by its possession of a unique set of natural abilities. This test is designed to help evaluate these natural abilities.

The test shall consist of two parts, (a) the approach to the quarry and (b) working the quarry. In order to qualify, a dog must pass both parts of the test.

Section 8. Junior Earthdog Test—Den Design. The den for the Junior Earthdog Test shall be constructed using the standard liners approximately nine (9) inches by nine (9) inches, set in such a manner as to provide a tunnel approximately 30 feet in length, with three 90 degree turns. The tunnel shall have an entrance at one end, and a quarry area at the other end, which shall provide the Judge a view of the dog during the working portion of the test. The dog should be removed from the den by way of the exit provided at the quarry end of the den. The den shall have no additional entrances, exits, or dead ends.

Section 9. Junior Earthdog Test—Qualifying Performance. Each dog shall be brought to the test area entrance by the handler who shall remove all leads, collars, harnesses, etc. before entering the test area. The handler shall carry the dog into the test area and stand at the designated starting point, a point directly in front of the den entrance at a distance of approximately 10 feet. Upon instructions from the Judge, the handler shall release the dog. The handler may, at the time of release, give the dog one short command with no penalty. The dog should be released no higher than waist level, and may be placed on the ground prior to release. Throwing the dog in the direction of the den entrance shall not be permitted, and shall cause the dog to fail. After releasing the dog, the handler shall quietly stand at the release point, with no further command or signal and shall not move, until instructed by the Judge. Further actions on the part of the handler during the time the dog is being tested could result in failure. The timing of the dog shall start when the dog is released by the handler. The dog has 30 seconds to reach the quarry. It may enter and leave the den without penalty, but must reach the quarry within the 30 second time limit. Dogs reaching the quarry within the 30 second time limit, which have not received any encouragement from the handler, shall pass this portion of the test.

Once the dog has reached the quarry it must remain with the quarry until the test is completed. Should the dog leave the quarry area during the test period it shall fail. The Judge shall allow the dog 30 seconds from the time it reached the quarry to begin working. If the dog fails to begin working within 30 seconds the dog shall fail this portion of the test.

The work must begin, and for the most part continue, at a point within one foot (12 inches) from the quarry. Once the dog begins working the quarry, it must work continuously for 60 seconds. Work shall be defined as barking, growling, digging, or any other form of activity which, in the Judge's opinion, indicates the dog's interest in the quarry. A change from one form of work to another shall not be considered as a break. Lunging and clearing dirt shall be considered work, as long as the dog stays with the quarry. Intense staring and/or sniffing the quarry should not be considered working. The Judge shall make no attempt to encourage the dog to work, or to continue to work. Dogs which work the quarry continuously for 60 seconds shall pass this portion of the test.

Upon completion of the test, the Judge should allow the handler to retrieve the dog from the earth. The dog should be removed by way of the top opening at the quarry end of the earth. The dog shall be carried from the test area as soon as possible, and not be allowed to investigate the test area.

The Judge shall mark the judging form with the time, indicating whether the dog passed or failed and may make written comments as provided on the form. The completed judging forms may be held by either the Judge's Steward or the Test Steward, and collected only by the Test Secretary.

At the completion of the test, the Judge shall announce the names of those dogs which have qualified. The test-giving club may award prizes or trophies to the qualifying dogs.

Section 10. Senior Earthdog Test. This test is designed to present the more experienced hunter with a more realistic den situation. In the wild, few natural earths are simple tunnels; they are complex, multiple entrance designs. The dog must be able to not only follow the quarry to ground and mark the game for the handler, but must also be able to determine the correct direction taken by the quarry. If the quarry has bolted (removed) the dog must leave the den when called by the hunter.

The Senior test shall consist of three parts: 1. The approach to the quarry; 2. Working the quarry; 3. Leaving the den on command.

Section 11. Senior Earthdog Test—Den Design. The den shall be constructed using the standard liners approximately nine (9) inches by nine (9) inches. The liners shall be set in such a manner as to provide a main tunnel approximately 30 feet in length, with three 90 degree turns, a false exit and false den. The false exit shall be approximately seven feet in length with one 90 degree turn and set in such a manner as to not be visible to the dog or handler when standing at the point of release.

The false den shall be a side tunnel with no exit, approximately four feet in length, with a twelve (12) inch by eight (8) inch door located at the top, not less than three inches from the end of the tunnel. Directly beneath the door shall be a pile of bedding material, i.e. straw, dry grass, heavily scented to simulate the litter/bedding area found in most natural dens.

The false exit and false den shall be set at the second and third 90 degree turn off the main tunnel, the order and placement of which shall be at the club's discretion. The entrance to the main tunnel shall be marked at a mound of dirt at least four inches higher than the top of the liner, thus providing a steep entrance to the den of at least a 45 degree incline into the earth. The dirt mound may be camouflaged by natural cover, provided the cover does not restrict entrance to the earth.

Section 12. Senior Earthdog Test—Qualifying Performance. Each dog shall be brought to the test area entrance by the handler who shall remove all leads, collars, harnesses, etc., before entering the test area. The handler shall carry the dog into the area and shall stand at the release point designated by the Judge (a point no less than 15 feet from the edge of the area, at a point marked by the Judge. This release point shall be approximately 20 feet from the entrance to the earth). Upon instruction from the Judge, the handler shall release the dog. The handler may, at the time of release, give the dog one short command with no penalty. The dog shall be released not higher than waist level, and may be placed on the ground before release. Throwing the dog in the direction of the den entrance shall not be permitted and shall cause the dog to fail. After releasing the dog, the handler shall quietly stand at the release point, with no further command or signal and shall not move, until instructed by the Judge.

Timing of the dog for the approach portion of the test shall start when the dog is released by the handler. The dog has 90 seconds from the time of release to reach the quarry, provided that it is continuously searching during that time. The dog may enter and leave the den, provided it has not reached the quarry. Once the dog has reached the quarry, it must remain with the quarry until the working portion of the test is completed. Should the dog leave the quarry area during the test it shall fail. The Judge shall allow the dog 15 seconds from the time it reached the quarry to begin working. If the dog fails to begin working within 15 seconds the dog shall not qualify.

Work shall be defined as barking, growling, digging or any other form of activity which, in the Judge's opinion, indicates the dog's interest in the quarry. A change from one form of work to another shall not be considered as a break. Lunging and clearing dirt shall be considered work. Intense staring and/or sniffing the quarry should not be considered working.

Once the dog has started to work, it must work the quarry for 90 seconds continuously. The Judge shall make no attempt to encourage the dog to work. Dogs that work for less than 90 seconds shall not pass.

Once the dog has completed the working portion of the test, the Judge shall seal the viewing area, remove the quarry and seal the quarry area, and have the caged quarry removed a sufficient distance so as not to be a distraction. The Judge shall then instruct the handler to recall the dog. The handler may go to the entrance of the den to call the dog, and may use a whistle. No bait, hides, noise-makers or toys may be used to recall the dog from the den. The handler is permitted to reach into the entrance of the den to retrieve the dog.

Dogs which exit the den (from any exit) and are retrieved by the handler within 90 seconds from the recall shall pass this portion of the test. The handler is positioned at the den entrance and may leave the den entrance to retrieve the dog once it has left the den. Dogs which exit the den in more than 90 seconds shall not pass.

The dog shall be carried from the test area as soon as possible, and should not be allowed to investigate the test area.

Dogs must pass all three parts of the test in order to qualify.

The Judge shall mark the judging form to indicate pass or fail, and may make written comments as provided on the form. The completed judging forms may be held by either the Judge's Steward or the Test Steward, and collected only by the Test Secretary.

At the completion of the test, the Judge shall announce the names of those dogs which have qualified. The testgiving club may award prizes or trophies to the dogs that have qualified.

Section 13. Master Earthdog Test. This test is designed to come as close as possible to a natural hunting situation. On a natural hunt, the dog is expected to locate the den and enter without encouragement. It should remain in the den working the quarry in a manner that will allow the hunter to locate both the dog and the quarry. If the quarry is unreachable by the hunter; e.g., in a rock den or a den located in a mountainside, or if the quarry is not to be taken by the hunter, the dog must leave the quarry and exit the den when called by the hunter.

Section 14. Master Earthdog Test—Den Design. The suggested Senior Earthdog tunnel is used for the Master test with modifications discussed below.

The den entrance shall not be readily visible, and shall be blocked with a removable obstruction. A scent line of approximately 20 feet shall lead to the entrance. An unscented false den entrance (visible to the dogs) is located midway along the scent line, at least five feet from the scent line. There must be a constriction point and an obstacle in the tunnel, either of which shall be placed within five feet of the entrance, or the quarry. The constriction point consists of boards or slats, approximately $1\frac{1}{2}$ inches wide, and 18 inches long, placed opposite each other to narrow the tunnel opening to approximately six inches. The ends of the boards or slats should be beveled or rounded. The obstruction should be a six-inch diameter PVC pipe placed crossways in the tunnel, and loosely mounted on a one-inch dowel so that it is movable (it should move approximately $2\frac{1}{2}$ inches each way). The portion of the liner above the obstruction (nine inches on each side of the center line, for a total of 18 inches) is elevated at least six inches over the main liner, and naturally camouflaged.

Section 15. Master Earthdog Test—Qualifying Performance. Dogs are worked two at a time. The braces shall be drawn at random, and whenever possible dogs owned by the same owner shall not be drawn to be worked together.

Handlers are positioned with the Judge and proceed in the direction of the scent line from the release point approximately 100 feet from the real den entrance. A Judge's Steward shall be positioned near the blocked den entrance to deal with overly aggressive dogs.

Dogs may investigate the false den, but must reach the real entrance before the Judge (generally the Judge should reach the den in about 60 seconds). Dogs barking the false den cannot qualify. Dogs must indicate the real tunnel entrance before the Judge reaches the tunnel entrance. If neither dog indicates the tunnel entrance, they cannot qualify, but can continue to be tested.

Prior to the removal of the entrance obstruction, each dog will have the opportunity to indicate interest in the entrance. If necessary, the first dog to reach and indicate the tunnel will be removed by the handler, and the second dog given the opportunity to indicate interest in the tunnel. The second dog is then staked approximately 10 feet from the tunnel entrance, using a twist-in ground type stake with a chain about two feet long (stake and chain are provided by the club).

A dog must reach the quarry within 90 seconds, and work the quarry for 90 seconds. When the dog is working the quarry, the Judge will create a distraction in the working area by lightly striking the top of the working area for 30 seconds with a piece of wood to simulate digging sounds. The dog should continue working and ignore the overhead distraction. The handler then removes the dog from the working area without injury to the handler.

The honoring dog will be collared with a flat buckle collar, and the handler will stay with the honoring dog and may caution the dog to be quiet. The dog must show interest, and may be occasionally vocal, but shall not bark continuously. The honoring dog is sent into the den when the working dog (first dog) is removed. The first dog then assumes the honor position (staked). The Judge and handler of the working dog are always positioned together.

Dogs must pass all parts of the test in order to qualify. The Judge shall mark the judging form to indicate pass or fail, and may make written comments as provided on the form. The completed judging forms may be held by either the Judges Steward or the Test Steward, and collected only by the Test Secretary.

At the completion of the test, the Judge shall announce the names of the dogs which have qualified. The test-giving club may award prizes or trophies to the dogs that have qualified.

Section 16. Testing a Bye-dog (the odd dog remaining at the end). Whenever there will be a bye-dog, the Test Committee may draw or otherwise select a bracemate from the dogs that have run, or use a dog that is not entered in the class. If one dog in a brace is excused for aggressiveness, the remaining dog is moved down to the bottom of the running order to run with the bye-dog (if there is no bye-dog, the foregoing methods will determine a bracemate). All dogs must be started with a bracemate, but never with a dog that will be under judgment at a later time.

AMERICAN KENNEL CLUB EARTHDOG BREEDS AND MORE

If there was only one universal truism about working earth-dog breeds it would probably be that, contrary to the old adage, a good big 'un rarely beats a good little 'un. In the den world, bigger is not better! Stuck in a hole, face to face and tooth to tooth with an ill-tempered adversary, maneuverability is a clear asset, while a large size is a definite hindrance.

The same is true of den trials. The nine-inch tall liner gives low-stationed breeds an obvious advantage over their taller cousins. No matter how you hack it, inadvertently or otherwise, the standard liner penalizes the taller breeds. When choosing a breed specifically for den work, one should remember that a nine-inch pipe is not the ideal size for a fifteen-inch dog. It is much like pouring a gallon of water into a pint jug, as the cliche goes. As if further proof were needed, of the 235 JE titles awarded in 1995, 75 recipients were Border Terriers and 73 were Dachshunds. Moreover, the same two breeds garnered all 18 SE title awards that year: Dachshunds had 12, Borders had six.

The significant difference between these two breeds is the huge gap between the breeds' annual AMERICAN KEN-NEL CLUB registration figures for 1995. Dachshunds placed eighth in overall popularity with a respectable 44,680

The principal regions of the British Isles—England, Scotland, Wales and Ireland—where most of the working terrier breeds are believed to have originated.

individual registrations. Border Terrier numbers were mighty stingy by comparison. The Border's 663 individual registrations—over 44,000 fewer than its rival—placed it at number 90 on the list, four notches below its rank for the previous year.

All of the breeds eligible for the AKC Earthdog Tests are listed below. (Rules governing AWTA, Jack Russells or other den tests or trials are available from their respective governing organizations.)

THE AUSTRALIAN TERRIER (3 SES)**

(Height: about 10 inches; weight: 12 to 14 pounds; 1995 registrations: 455)

---

* Breeds owned by the author; ** breeds handled by the author; figures in parentheses indicate the number of Junior and Senior Earthdog titles awarded to each breed in 1995, the first full year American Kennel Club Earthdog titles were issued.

The Australian Terrier was developed to suit the particular needs of British settlers to Australia using an effective combination of excellent working terrier types, such as the Dandie Dinmont and Yorkshire.

Known in Australia since 1885, the Aussie is one of many terrier breeds thought to be descended in part from the extinct Old English Black-and-Tan or Broken-haired Terrier. Other ancestors may include the Dandie Dinmont, Skye, Scottish, Irish and Cairn Terriers. The Yorkshire Terrier is also a likely contributor to the mix.

Recognized by the American Kennel Club in 1960, the alert, spirited little Aussie was originally used as a ratter, hedge-hunter and mine guard in the Australian outback. His small size and great speed made him especially adept at dispatching snakes; an important asset in his country of origin. The majority of today's Aussies have retained the spirit and determination needed to become formidable earth-dog prospects.

The older type Bedlington Terrier was possibly better suited to den work than some of its flashier descendants. This is a Bedlington champion of 1950s vintage—not that different from today's dogs, but not that similar either.

Because of the breed's size disadvantage, Bedlington Terrier owners and their dogs may choose to sleep on the AKC's offer to include them in Earthdog Tests in their existing format. Actually, Bedlingtons make effective earthdogs, but their primary sporting use was in coursing rabbits and racing.

THE BEDLINGTON TERRIER (ZERO)

(Height: dogs, 16½ inches, bitches, 15½ inches; weight: from 17 to 25 pounds, proportionate to size; 1995 registrations: 213)

The deceptive, lamb-like appearance of the Bedlington Terrier completely belies its legendary gameness. For many years the Bedlington was the favorite sporting terrier of the coal miners, nail makers and gypsies of Northumberland in the north of England.

First shown in the late 1800s, the versatile Bedlington was used for ratting, rabbit coursing, ferreting, poaching, racing, and in the pits. Despite its many sterling qualities, the Bedlington may prove to be too tall for earthdog tests.

THE BORDER TERRIER (74 JES, 6 SES)**

(Height: not specified; weight: dogs, 13 to 15½ pounds, bitches, 11½ to 14 pounds; 1995 registrations: 663).

The hardy, no-nonsense Border Terrier was developed in the Cheviot Hills between England and Scotland solely for its working qualities. Shepherds, farmers, smallholders and sportsmen came to appreciate the breed's strength, endurance and courage.

Formerly used to find foxes and other vermin, and protect livestock from predators, the Border is fast gaining a reputation as a premier earthdog. A couple of Border Terriers were among the first to be awarded American Kennel Club earthdog titles.

THE CAIRN TERRIER (6 JES)*

(Height: 9½ to 10 inches; weight: 13 to 14 pounds; 1995 registrations: 4,102)

Possibly one of the oldest of Scotland's terrier breeds, the Cairn has a long history and is considered a true working terrier. At one time, Cairns hunted otters, foxes, and other vermin inhabiting the rugged terrain characteristic of the Isle of Skye and the northern Highlands. He needed great courage to face the creatures that sought refuge in the piles of rocks, or

Determination fairly exudes from this Border Terrier as he makes his way toward the quarry.

cairns, from which the breed derived its name. While not usually called upon to seek vermin in the present, the qualities that helped the breed excel at this work are still present in today's Cairn. A small, active, tenacious worker, conformation-wise the Cairn is well suited to Earthdog Tests. The owner? Maybe not.

The much-loved Cairn Terrier is blessed with all the attributes required to excel at den work. This is the memorable Cairn standout, Am., Can. Ch. Woody Woodpecker of Melita, with the author, who handled him to a successful show career.

All three varieties of Dachshund frequently participate at both AKC and AWTA den trials.

THE DACHSHUND VARIETIES—LONGHAIRED, SMOOTH, WIREHAIRED (73 JES, 12 SES) **

(Weight: Standard, over 11 pounds; Miniature, 11 pounds and under; 1995 registrations: 44,680. See Chapter 5 for more details.)

THE DANDIE DINMONT TERRIER (ZERO)**

(Height: 8 to 11 inches; weight: 18 to 24 pounds; 1995 registrations: 78)

Another product of the English-Scottish border, the unique Dandie Dinmont Terrier was once used to hunt all manner of vermin, from rats and weasels to foxes, badgers and otters. The breed was thought to have been first portrayed in a 1770 Gainsborough portrait of Henry, third Duke of Buccleuch. However, that bit of history depends on the eye of the beholder.

In 1814 Sir Walter Scott, himself a proud owner and great admirer of the breed, wrote the novel *Guy Mannering* in which the character Dandie Dinmont, a farmer, boasted that he pitted his terriers against rats, weasels, foxes, and badgers and

This etching of the Dandie Dinmont Terrier, "Border Queen," appeared in Charles Cook's landmark 1885 book on the breed. The breed has changed little since the end of the 19th century.

Handled properly, today's Dandie is quite adept at den work. The soft eyes and silky topknot belie a truly game terrier.

"that now they fear naething that ever cam' wi a hairy skin on't." To which the author added in his notes: "The race of Pepper and Mustard are in the highest estimation at the present day not only for vermin killing, but for intelligence and fidelity . . . ."

If spirit, energy, tenacity and downright hard-headed stubbornness are any assets for successful participation in Earthdog Tests, Dandies have all of that and more. All that is required is for owners to give their dogs a try, and these folks would be in for a pleasant surprise.

THE FOX TERRIER VARIETIES—SMOOTH, WIRE (SMOOTH, 18 JES; WIRE, 12 JES) *

(Height: 15½ inches or less; weight: 16 to 18 pounds; 1995 registrations: Smooth, 945; Wire, 2,118)

This modern Smooth Fox Terrier champion smells a rat . . . or several!

The Wire Fox Terrier, a long-time favorite, is considered by many the "classic terrier." Although the Standard itself has changed little, the sloping topline and high withers of present-day Fox Terriers vary greatly from those of its early ancestors.

(NEW TYPE) WIREHAIRED FOXTERRIER CH. ROPER'S NUT-CRACK". SIR H. DE TRAFFORD BT. OWNER.

This is an illustration of a turn-of-the-century English Wire Fox Terrier, Ch. Roper's Nut-Crack, owned by Sir H. De Trafford. Classified at the turn of the century as a representative of the "the new type," this Wire clearly demonstrates the dramatic evolution of the breed over the past 100 years.

Smooth and Wire Fox Terriers are both venerable English breeds formerly regarded in the United States as two varieties of the same breed. This historic division into separate breeds went into effect in 1985. Smooths were first exhibited in their homeland in 1862, with Wires entering the arena some 15 years later.

Surprisingly, the original standard, drawn up in 1876 by the Fox Terrier Club of England, has hardly changed over the years. That's not to say dramatic changes have not occurred in that time, however.

Highly regarded by huntsmen the world over, the original Fox Terriers became the favorites with English hunters because of their immense desire to go to ground and unearth foxes. Today's Fox Terriers may be a bit tall for nine inch liners, but they otherwise posses abundant potential to excel as earthdogs.

THE LAKELAND TERRIER (2 JES) *

(Height: approx. 14½ inches; weight: approx. 17 pounds; 1995 registrations: 228.)

The Lakeland Terrier originated in the Fell district of Cumberland, England—not far from the Scottish border—and home to a strain of large, fierce hill foxes. Like other broken-coated terriers, the Lakeland has a hard, wiry outer coat and soft, warm undercoat as protection against the cold and dampness of their native land. The breed is said to be related to the Welsh, Airedale, and possibly the Bedlington Terriers.

An accomplished swimmer, the Lakeland is among the oldest working terriers used to exterminate otters, foxes and other vermin. Still bred in small numbers, the breed has retained many of the better qualities most valued by earth-dog folks.

Author Mario Migliorini's Lakeland Terrier, Ch. Rubin of Char-Dar. The Lakeland is one of the long-legged terriers that is still well-adapted to the demands of modern den trials.

A present-day, working Lakeland Terrier: no frills—anywhere.

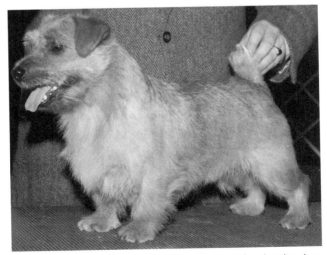

The Norfolk Terrier's size makes this breed ideal for den work and modern dogs are up to the challenge of the terrier's calling. The model here is William J. Mott's Ch. Surrey Spinnaker. *William Gilbert*

THE NORFOLK TERRIER (ZERO)

(Height: 10 inches; weight: 11 to 12 pounds; 1995 registrations: 297)

These hardy little terriers first appeared in England around 1880. Developed in stables in Cambridge, for a time they were a favorite with sporting Cambridge University undergraduates, who called them Cantab Terriers.

When this fearless, active terrier proved to be very useful during fox hunts, it soon became a firm favorite of local huntsmen. Truly, the Norfolk Terrier is ideally suited for earthdog sports.

THE NORWICH TERRIER (2 JES)

(Height: 10 inches; weight: 11 to 12 pounds; 1995 registrations: 388)

Norwich Terriers, such as this fine pair of champions owned by Karen Whalen, make perfect earthdog prospects.

Bred from a variety of native, Yorkshire and Irish den stock, the Norwich are thought to be the diminutive descendants of a notorious ratter named "Rags" said to carry the genes of a "miniature" Staffordshire Terrier. One can only assume the term was used to imply the Staff was significantly undersize.

Used both for ratting and bolting foxes, they are first cousins to the Norfolk Terrier. The most obvious difference between the two breeds is ear carriage: drop-eared in the Norfolk, prick-eared in the Norwich. Prior to 1964 in Great Britain and 1979 in the United States, both breeds were shown as Norwich. Today the two are shown separately wherever these personable red earth dogs are known.

THE SCOTTISH TERRIER (9 JES) *
(Height: approx. 10 inches; weight: 18 to 22 pounds; 1995 registrations: 5,311.)

Conflicting stories abound concerning the antiquity of the Scottish Terrier. First given its own classes at Birmingham, England in 1860, the first pair of the breed arrived in the United States around 1883.

There are numerous theories on the origin of the breed. Some authorities suggest the Scottish Terrier is descended from the original Skye Terriers, a breed nothing like the Skye of today. That ancestor probably more closely resembled modern Cairns.

The Scottie was once the firm favorite of some professional fox hunters; the hounds would pursue the fox, running it to ground, and the Scottie would follow the game to ground. Having exceptionally powerful jaws, for many years the breed was highly prized for baiting* and drawing foxes. Compact and built low to the ground, with great strength

* "Baiting" was a spectator sport in which dogs attacked or worried captured prey. "Drawing" required a dog to grab hold of a fox or badger so the handler could draw or extract them from the den while they were locked in each others jaws.

Illustrated here is a turn-of-the-century Scottish Terrier. Staunch individualists and fiercely independent, not all Scotties may be equally well-suited to advanced Earthdog Tests as are some of the other breeds eligible for the activity.

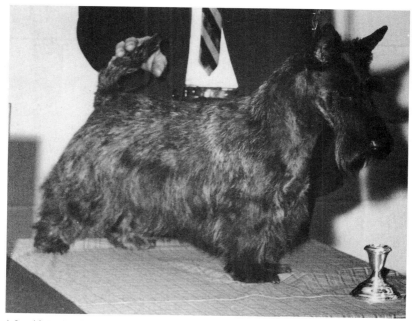

A Scottish Terrier of more recent vintage equally capable of winning and working.

55

and digging ability, the Scottie is renowned for its keen nose, good vision, acute hearing and the desire to hunt and dig for vermin.

THE SEALYHAM TERRIER (ZERO)

(Height: 10½ inches; weight: 23 to 24 pounds; 1995 registrations: 108)

This dog was originally bred to hunt the fox, badger, and otter in packs or individually. The Sealyham Terrier was created by Captain John Edwards and named after his Sealyham estate near Haverfordwest in Wales. In the mid-1800s, Edwards attempted to perfect the Sealy as a breed with endurance and unsurpassed gameness. It was first shown in Wales in 1903, in England in 1910, and registered by the American Kennel Club in 1911.

An even-tempered breed with a pleasing disposition, the Sealyham was developed with the makings of an exceptional den dog. Unfortunately, like several other earthdog breeds,

The Sealyham Terrier is a product of the 19th century and was developed in Wales specifically as an earthdog of peerless courage and ability.

the overall Sealyham population is very small—too much for the breed's own good.

THE SKYE TERRIER (ZERO) **

(Height: 10 inches; length: 20 inches; weight: in proportion; 1995 registrations: 84)

Although this is not everyone's favorite terrier breed, the Skye has the necessary qualities to make him a good earth-dog. Even so, it may be a very long time before Skyes are a common sight at Earthdog Tests. The size of today's Skye Terriers makes them somewhat unsuited to present-day den work.

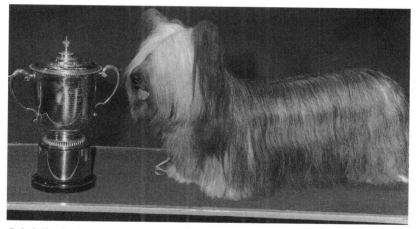

Today's Skye Terrier may be better suited to the show ring than to Earthdog Tests. Time will tell!

WELSH TERRIER (8 JES) *

(Height: approx. 15 inches; weight: approx. 20 pounds; 1995 registrations: 556)

Believed by some authorities to be the original Old English Wirehaired Black-and-Tan Terrier, the Welsh can claim great antiquity. Like most of the smaller terriers, the Welsh was formerly used to hunt and exterminate otter, fox, badger and other small vermin. Little changed since first

The modern Welsh Terrier has the required talent; however, its larger size may prove a handicap at Earthdog Tests.

This is an old-time "Welshman" of years past. Note this dog's obvious similarity to the early Wire Fox Terrier from the same era shown earlier in this chapter.

shown in Caernarvon in 1885, the "Welshman" has the true qualities of a fine earthdog. However, much like some of the other high-stationed terriers, when compared with the shorter-legged breed he is somewhat unfairly handicapped at having to force his 15-inch height into a nine-inch tunnel liner.

THE WEST HIGHLAND WHITE TERRIER (28 JES)

(Height: 10 to 11 inches; weight, in proportion; 1995 registrations: 7,772)

The Westie has long been the most popular going-to-ground terrier breed in the United States. A hardy, energetic hunter, the Westie is believed to have originated in Poltalloch, Scotland, and is closely related to the Cairn. Others concede he may have originated from the same basic stock, but maintain he is not directly related. Regardless of his true origin, the lively Westie is a dynamic hunter and has shown himself to be an exceptional earthdog candidate.

The West Highland White Terrier, typically so *full of himself*, is of the correct size, ability and disposition to participate successfully at all Earthdog Tests. This "Westie," Ch. Dawn's Kop N' A Plea, SE, CG, owned and bred by Dawn L. Martin and Patricia H. Marks has achieved success in the show ring and as a capable earthdog.

OTHER ABLE EARTHDOG BREEDS

As of yet, the American Kennel Club does not recognize all the highly regarded den breeds. The most conspicuous absentee is the demon of the dens, the Jack Russell Terrier and to a lesser extent, the Patterdale Terrier; the Deutscher

The Jack Russell Terrier, as yet not recognized by AKC, is rated highest among today's elite working earthdogs in Great Britain and around the world. Unfortunately, individuals may range in size from ten to fifteen inches at the withers. A possible size differential of 50% is a bit unrealistic for working terrier breeds. *Carlo Corby*

Jagdterrier (German Hunt); the Glen of Imaal Terrier; Cesky (Czech) Terrier; and—in my singular opinion—the Yorkshire Terrier.

Although ineligible for any kind of award or recognition of accomplishment, at most digs, participation by "unrecognized" breeds is generally permitted "for exhibition only." Meaning, they are allowed to run after the official test activities have been concluded, just for the hell of it.

The Yorkshire Terrier*
(Height: not specified; weight: 7 pounds or less)

In 1874, the first Yorkie was entered in the Kennel Club Stud Book in England under the dual names "Broken-haired Scotch or Yorkshire Terrier." Originally, the diminutive Yorkie was bigger then he is today, but not by much. The fact is, he remains the same spirited fireball, ready and willing to tackle all comers, including those many times his size. Legend has it that one of the principle functions of early Yorkshire Terriers was to protect their owners from being attacked by rats while they slept. Yorkies were considered exceptional ratters; some still are.

In my opinion, based on past accounts the Yorkie should be included in the American Kennel Club's official list of earthdog eligibles. I suggest this little dynamo makes a better candidate than some of the breeds that made the list. My wife's Yorkie, Skipper, is the perfect example of their scrappy spirit. In fact, I was compelled to find a new home for my chunky-type Xoloitzcuintili (the equal of any Staffordshire Terrier), because my wife's Yorkie simply refused to back down from the bigger, younger, stronger Mexican Hairless. There was never a doubt in my mind that the courageous, stubborn little Yorkie would put his life on the line once too often by harassing his stronger companion. One thing is certain, "Skipper" was eager to go to ground and worked quarry better than most terriers I've known. Having owned, bred or handled a large number of credible terrier champions, I know whereof I speak!

Like numerous other breeds, Yorkshires were intended to have a utilitarian purpose; in this case, as efficient ratters. Before long, proud or boastful owners felt the need to prove whose was the best ratter. Consequently, "ratting" soon became a favorite diversion of both the working class and so-called "sporting gentlemen"—another name for gamblers before the turn of the century.

Terriers were paired off, one against another, to determine which of the two could dispatch a given number of rats in the

Margaret Migliorini's Yorkshire terrier, "Skipper," was a Master Earthdog in every sense of the word. Many Yorkshires, just like Skipper, prove that this breed deserves the chance to show it is a great deal more than a longhaired lap dog.

shortest elapsed time. An agreed-upon number of newly-trapped sewer or wharf rats were counted and released into an enclosure or pit, whereupon the dogs took turns at catching and killing them as swiftly as possible.

The following excerpt from Robert Leighton's *The Complete Book of the Dog* illustrates this well:

> The local pub was a likely place to see good sport. As time went on, rats became less easy to obtain and it became fashionable to run handicaps. These were arranged so that the heavier the dog was the more rats he had to kill.
>
> Various handicaps were set ranging from one rat being added to a dog's quota for every three pounds of additional weight over his rival, to one rat for every pound. This was perhaps the favorite and it was frequent to arrange a handicap where each dog had to kill as many rats as there were pounds in his weight. The dog disposing of his quota the quickest being the winner. *This put rather a premium on small dogs and breeds were developed especially for this sport.* The Smooth Black-and-Tan Terriers of Manchester and the rough Yorkshire Terriers were particularly good for this sport.

Initially at least, it was this type of competition that encouraged breeders to reduce the Yorkie's size.

An interesting account from the mid-1960s explains how a four-pound Yorkie cleared an English apple orchard of rabbits. The tale sounds typical of an average country terrier, no matter the breed:

> Although only four pounds, Tidy [a Yorkshire Terrier] was as tough as nails. She took charge of fourteen acres of rabbit-infested orchard, which were like a wilderness, and bolted 129 rabbits in less than three

months. On one occasion she could not be gotten out [of the warren] and they had to dig for her. When she was reached, there were five dead rabbits and Tidy herself calmly sitting on a tree root.

On another occasion she spotted a rabbit; off she went after it, over a field onto a frozen brook covered with thin ice. Down she went but emerged on the other side, shook herself and then continued on.

Rats were always marked and she would not move before her owner had dug them out.

Her greatest joy was the old village poacher. They knew each other like buddies. Tidy could smell him a mile off [no comment]. She would sit on the window-sill trembling in anticipation, awaiting his approach. The moment she saw him she would hop off her perch, dash out and jump into his pocket and off these two would go for a day's sport. Tidy always brought dinner home for the other dogs.

THE OLD ENGLISH BROKEN-HAIRED BLACK-AND-TAN TERRIER: GONE BUT NOT FORGOTTEN

Exactly when, where, why, and how the first true terriers evolved will always be a mystery. Speculation is plentiful, but consensus overwhelmingly favors the Old English Broken-haired Black-and-Tan Terrier as the principle progenitor and genetic cornerstone of most modern terrier breeds.

For many generations, Welsh Terrier fanciers have been eager to bestow this distinction on their favorite, and not completely without justification. For a time, the Welsh Terrier and the Old English Broken-haired Black-and-Tan were virtually indistinguishable except for size. During a period of seventeen months, leading up to April 1887, the two breeds were entered in the Kennel Club (England) Stud Book under the joint classification: "Welsh Terrier *or* Old English Broken-haired Black-and-Tan Terrier, Class Number 53."

To further complicate the issue, a grizzle and tan Old English Broken-haired Black-and-Tan Terrier named Dick

An artist's impression of an Old English Broken-haired Black-and-Tan Terrier as it may have looked prior to 1895, before ear cropping was banned in England. Note the white chest characteristic of the breed at that time.

An artist's impression of a hard-eyed Old English Broken-haired Black-and-Tan as the breed might have looked in the 1920s.

Turpin was successfully exhibited at the same show and awarded prizes, first as a Welsh and then as an Old English Broken-haired Black-and-Tan Terrier.

Named for a notorious highwayman, Dick Turpin is known to have changed ownership at least four times. With each ownership change the dog was reclassified, first as one breed and then as the other.

In July, 1893, Harold M. Bryans (owner number four) chose to enter the dog at Darlington in both Welsh and Old English Black-and-Tan breed classes under two different judges, each a breed expert in his own right. Dick Turpin was awarded first place in the Welsh Terrier class, after which he placed fourth as an Old English Broken-haired Black-and-Tan Terrier. It was an unprecedented occurrence, even a hundred years ago. Inaccurate accounts surfaced from time to time suggesting Dick Turpin placed first in both of these classes, but these have long since been discredited.

Although the generic Old English Broken-haired Black-and-Tan Terrier is now extinct, he remains one of the most likely early ancestors of our diverse present-day terrier breeds. However, when and where the Old English Broken-haired Black-and-Tan Terrier originated will probably always remain a mystery.

Not everyone has enthusiastically embraced this same theory over the years. Walter S. Glynn, a knowledgeable turn-of-the-century writer and loyal Welsh Terrier fancier, was one of them. Convinced of the Old English Broken-haired Black-and-Tan's ignoble heritage, Glynn unequivocally labeled the breed a non–self-reproducing hybrid, or a mule of sorts, when he wrote:

> It is not surprising he [the Old English Black-and-Tan] could not beget himself, for at no show was he exhibited as an Old English Broken-haired Terrier, by an Old English Broken-haired Terrier, out of an Old English Broken-haired Terrier.

There is evidence that they [the Old English Black-and-Tans] were manufactured from all sorts of breeds, which all contributed their quota.

Contrary to Glynn's adverse opinion, the Old English Broken-haired Black-and-Tan remains the most widely acknowledged early ancestor of today's wirehaired breeds, the Manchester Terrier and others, including the diminutive Yorkshire Terrier.

In comparison to Glynn's blatant assault on its genetic integrity, Dr. William Bruette was decidedly more appreciative of the breed. In *The Complete Dog Book* (1924), he expressed his appreciation of the Old English Broken-haired Black-and-Tan with these words:

This ancient English breed of working terrier is one of a few for which a specialist club does not exist, and there is a decided call for one to save it from utter extinction. A quarter of a century must have elapsed since a specimen of this breed [Old English Broken-haired Black-and-Tan] was exhibited. As a kennel terrier the Old English is prominent in the history of country sport, and he is doubtless the progenitor of the more popular and plentiful Fox Terrier.

The Old English Broken-haired Black-and-Tan Terrier is a dog of great antiquity. He appears in some of the oldest prints and paintings, and no sportsman's establishment of olden times was considered complete without him. Today his ranks are thinned even in the hunting field, whilst he is nearly unknown on the show bench.

Such a sterling terrier in make and shape and hardihood and grit should not be allowed to lapse into obscurity [make that oblivion]. No breed, either from the point of view of antiquity, tradition, appearance, and utility was or is more fitting of

The *Deutscher Jagdterrier*, or German Hunt Terrier, might be the closest surviving relative of the extinct Old English Broken-haired Black-and-Tan.

perpetuation. Those who know agree that they possess the traits to be cherished in the hearts of everyone who loves a dog for his worth and not for what he would fetch in the market.

The chief differences between the Old English and the Welsh Terriers are in the size, the latter being a few pounds heavier. The Old English Terrier has a long, strong, punishing jaw, level mouth, flat skull, free from cheekiness, and a small, dark, determined eye; good bone, coat hard to the touch; colors, black-and-tan and grizzle and tan.

Barely a decade later, a book containing the Official Standards of all the terrier breeds recognized by the Kennel Club in England made no mention of the breed. In all probability, the Old English Broken-haired Black-and-Tan's closest descendant might be the *Deutscher Jagdterrier*, or German Hunt Terrier.

The Jagdterrier, whose common appearance belies his game reputation, is regarded as an exceptionally tough and extremely aggressive hunting dog with great keenness for going to ground. Considered somewhat unsuitable as a house dog by those who know him well, the German Hunt Terrier is a highly regarded hunter and was developed in the early 1930s, at about the same time the Old English Broken-haired Black-and-Tan Terrier drifted quietly into extinction.

DER DACHSHUND

First mentioned in print around the late 1600s and early 1700s, and referred to favorably in Johann Tanzer's *Jagdgeheimnissen* (Secrets of Hunting) in 1734, the Dachshund is easily traceable to the 1560s from woodcuts of the period depicting Dachshund-like dogs with long bodies, short legs and houndy ears, engaged in various stages of tracking quarry that apparently had gone to ground.

According to prominent authorities, carvings of low stationed dogs resembling Dachshunds were discovered in early Egyptian tombs dating back 4,000 to 5,000 years or more. Recent evidence suggests a possibility that the earliest ancestors of present-day Dachshunds may actually predate the Bronze Age.

First used to unearth small game by the Romans, Greeks and ultimately the Prussians, recent archeological finds suggest that the Old German Dachshund may be traced back to the ancient *Canis sagaces*, the cold-trailing black hounds bred by the Benedictine Monks at their monastery in the Ardennes—early ancestors of many modern hounds via the Celtic Hound and its subsequent descendants.

A favorite of German and Austrian nobles and their foresters, the Dachshund boasts a long, proud history as an accomplished hunter and fearless den dog. Its progenitors may have accompanied the mounted falconers of the Middle Ages who preferred slow-moving hounds to the faster, long-legged varieties that ranged too far ahead to be of practical value to falconers.

Illustrated here is a Wirehaired Dachshund (above) and a Longhaired specimen. A Smooth Dachshund is shown on p. 46. All three Dachshund varieties have more than proven their ability as earthdogs.

Capable of hunting alone or in packs, the versatile *Dachswurger* or "badger strangler" was as equally at home going to ground to bolt the fox or draw the badger as it was trailing a wild boar and deer in the Black Forest.

The breed was introduced into Great Britain by Prince Albert of Saxe-Coburg, the Prince Regent, following his marriage to Queen Victoria. Records indicate that the Dachshund was recognized in Great Britain in 1874, and entered in the German Stud book in 1879 and the AKC Stud book in 1885.

The first definitive book on the breed was Emil Ilgner's *Der Dachshund,* published in 1896—fully seventeen years after the so-called "racial characteristics" (or standards) for the breed were compiled in 1879.

Over the long period of their popularity, Dachshunds have been referred to by a variety of names; some serious, some tongue-in-cheek. One prominent German authority on the breed was sufficiently provoked by the apparent inability of Americans to pronounce the breed's name correctly, that he devoted an entire page in his book to explaining that the correct pronunciation is *dacks-hoont.*

Dachs is German for badger; *hund* means dog, but not necessarily "hound." The confusion between "hund" and "hound" remains annoyingly prevalent in dog books written in English. The name simply means "badger dog"; however, the breed was never restricted to hunting the badger or any other single species.

The modern Dachshund is generally believed to have developed around the mid-sixteenth century from cross-breedings of little-known hound types. These were made by foresters and game keepers in the employ of sports-minded members of the German/Prussian aristocracy.

Perhaps by chance, a number of similar, low-stationed breeds appears to have evolved in Switzerland, France, Germany, and parts of Scandinavia within a relatively short time of each other. This short-legged anomaly is attributed to a hereditary malformation of the bones known as *achondroplasia*. Whether this development happened by chance or the breeds that emerged were somehow interrelated will always remain a matter of pure speculation. The most notable of the short-legged hounds are the Basset Hound and Petit Basset Griffon Vendeen, Short-legged Schweisshund, Swedish Dachsbracke, the Bernese Short-legged Hound, and the Jura Hound. There can be little doubt that some of these were used to develop the first Dachshunds.

When Mrs. Henry B. Lent, Jr., founded the American Working Terrier Association, she indicated that the main objective of the AWTA was to enable terrier owners to take their dogs into the field and develop their natural terrier instincts under relatively safe conditions. Giving terriers an opportunity to hunt aboveground in a controlled environment, where little or no harm might befall them was the primary objective. Originally it was hoped that at least some participants would go to ground.

Acknowledging that the Dachshund, known in Germany as the *Deutscher Teckel,* is equally as qualified and capable of denwork as any working terrier, Dachshund owners were invited to join the AWTA in 1972 and participate at AWTA events. They did so with great success and since that time participation and interest in earthdog activities by Dachshund owners has exceeded all expectations.

The year 1985 marked a memorable step towards rekindling the Dachshund's renowned reputation for versatility in the field. That year the breed was given its first opportunity to compete in an unprecedented five disciplines, including: bench, obedience, tracking, field and den. The AWTA Den Trial, judged by Karla Martin, took place at the Old Redmond Golf Course in Redmond, Washington, in early July of that year. The Highest Scoring Dachshund in Trial was a first-time participant that came from the Novice B class, Am., Can.

Ch. Lilliputian Singing Low MS, TD—otherwise known as "Spooky."

Owned by Susan Krinder and Pat Walker, Spooky qualified and competed in the Open class, earning her Certificate of Gameness. That, in turn, gave Spooky a free trip to the Certificate class, where her time of seven and a half seconds was good enough to edge out the ten-year-old veteran, Fld. Ch. Natasha of Bagerbane, for top honors by a mere half second!

In 1994 the American Kennel Club introduced its version of Earthdog Tests, with the emphasis on den work. Fortunately for Dachshund owners, the AKC's directors had the foresight to include the Dachshund in its list of breeds eligible to participate in this exciting performance event.

Although the Dachshund's name is not specifically mentioned in each chapter of this book, most of the contents apply equally to Dachshunds and eligible terrier breeds alike.

The author readily acknowledges the valuable contribution of Dachshunds and their owners to the success of AWTA Den Trials over the years. However, identifying specific terrier breeds and Dachshunds by name throughout the text would have been needlessly cumbersome; no discrimination is implied or intended.

There is no doubt that Dachshund fanciers will contribute greatly to the future success of the AKC's Earthdog Tests program. Not only were nine of the first fifteen dogs to attain AKC Earthdog titles Dachshunds, they also accounted for two thirds of the Senior Earthdog titles awarded in 1995. That speaks for itself.

UNDERSTANDING THE BADGER

Legend has it the modern Dachshund was developed specifically to confront and draw the badger from its sett, or den.

Although generally regarded as omnivorous, the surly, ill-tempered badger is mostly vegetarian. Pound for pound, the brock—or grey as he is also known in Great Britain—rates as one of the most tenacious and potentially dangerous adversaries a dog might be called upon to face.

Confronted above ground, a 30- to 40-pound badger can prostrate itself so low to the ground, it can look almost as flat as the proverbial pancake. This low center of gravity allows the badger to cling to the ground like a giant suction cup. Not only does this maneuver protect its most vulnerable parts, it makes the badger extremely difficult to attack or immobilize.

On the other hand, this low profile permits the badger to sweep the legs out from under its taller opponents at lightning speed and with surprising ease. Once off their feet, would-be aggressors become easy victims to the badger's punishing bombardment of teeth and claws.

The badger has no natural enemies. His fellow creatures in the wild, big and small alike, are happy to give him a long look and a wide berth.

There are badger setts in existence, undisturbed by man, which are said to have remained occupied consistently for as long as one hundred years. A few of the oldest are comprised of an intricate maze of tunnels. It is estimated that when combined, these tunnels extend a mile or more beneath the adjacent countryside.

IDEALLY EQUIPPED

It is not unreasonable to assume that a dog capable of challenging this formidable adversary would itself be equally courageous and aggressive. Early Dachshunds were all of that.

A 1912 description of hunting Dachshunds concludes as follows: "They are snappy, pugnacious, brave but often quarrelsome animals, who are tenacious for life. They tend to start fights with any dog, no matter how large he is." That was then; this is now!

The Dachshund's conformation, the butt of endless jokes over the years, is actually an anatomical marvel. Should it be necessary, its chest (or keel) can serve a similar function as a skid, or runner on a sled, enabling the dog to slide or maneuver himself in and out of tight spots. He is also able to take his full weight on his chest, freeing his legs for digging. His loose, angular shoulder assembly allows him to tuck his legs close into his body for maximum mobility in confined spaces.

In addition to providing ample heart and lung capacity, his large diaphragm and extended rib cage provide essential support for his unusually long back. An angular hind assembly enables the Dachshund to creep along subterranean lairs, or pursue his quarry above ground with equal ease. The long head, supported by a powerful neck, is equipped with punishing jaws and strong teeth—weapons equally well suited for attack or defense.

Finally, should the need arise, the Dachshund's long straight tail, extended horizontally behind him, provides a convenient handle for a hunter to grasp and forcibly extricate a Dachshund that is stuck in a hole. This last modification on a superb digging machine eliminates the need to resort to a pick and shovel.

In Germany, the Dachshund is known by several names including *Dackel and Teckel.* But, perhaps the most interesting variation is *Kaninchentekel,* or rabbit dog, used to classify the smaller varieties. This seems to indicate that Dachshunds, like most terriers, were used as pot hunters to provide meat for the table as much as they were used for recreation.

One of the less appealing aspects of putting dogs to ground has always been the prospect of having to dig them out later. Fortunately, Earthdog Tests have eliminated this chore—more or less. These days, the digging is done ahead of time in order to bury the den liners in preparation for the trials.

Dachshund Field Trials, conducted for the purpose of obtaining a Field Championship may also require a Dachshund to follow its quarry to ground. However, since Field Trials per se are not germane to this book, additional details have been omitted.

For more information and a copy of the rules governing Dachshund Field Trials, or any other pertinent information, contact the American Kennel Club, or the secretary of the local Dachshund Club nearest you.

BUYING AN EARTHDOG PUPPY

Anyone contemplating buying a puppy for the first time should learn a few basic facts before, rather than after, making such an important and long-term commitment. When buying any puppy, it is best to be aware of what its primary function is: pet, companion, watchdog, show dog, earthdog, or whatever. The puppy is then selected primarily on that basis. Leave as little as possible to chance.

PUREBRED OR ILL-BRED?

Unfortunately, many first-time owners do not understand the significance (or insignificance) of terms like "pedigreed," "purebred," "AKC registered," "championship-bred," "beautifully marked," or similar confusing terminology.

"Pedigreed" simply indicates that the dog has a documented genealogical list of names presumed to be those of the puppy's ancestors. The average pedigree goes back three or four generations—parents, grandparents and great-grandparents. All too often, however, these names may have little or no significance to the real worth of the dog to which they pertain.

Pedigrees should contain the names of all champions of record on both the dam's and sire's side. These names should also include any degrees from performance events that any of a dog's ancestors may have earned.

These Jack Russell Terrier puppies from a good, working strain illustrate that, quality aside, healthy puppies should be plump, bright-eyed and friendly.

An impressive pedigree, by itself, is no proof of individual quality. However, it does suggest that a certain amount of "quality control" was exercised when it mattered most.

"Purebred" means a dog's ancestors were of the same breed for a given number of generations. A dog may be purebred, but not eligible for AKC registration: e.g., if one or both the parents have no "papers." There are lots of these dogs around.

"AKC registered" means the breeder has done the necessary paperwork and paid the required fee. In return for this, the American Kennel Club will first register the entire litter and, upon receipt of an official individual application and fee, will issue a certificate of registration for any given dog. Under normal circumstances, all offspring from AKC registered parents—regardless of quality—are eligible for AKC registration, period.

"Championship bred" has a ring similar to "genuine imitation." I suspect it means to imply there may be champion ancestors lurking somewhere way, way back in the dog's genealogy. This term is frequently used in classified ads when there is little else to say.

Keep in mind that these official-sounding terms do not guarantee a puppy's quality, even when a puppy is AKC-registered. AKC is not a trademark; it does not represent or imply any special degree of perfection. New owners may wrongly believe that once they purchase an AKC-registered or AKC-registrable puppy, they have acquired something special, maybe a future champion. Not in this lifetime!

Being "AKC-registered" is only one of many requirements of a prospective show dog. Above all, the dog must conform to the specific requirements outlined in its official breed Standard.

Show quality Welsh (left) and Lakeland Terrier puppies with noted breeders Darlene and Chuck Paynter. The dollar value of working, companion and show-quality specimens varies greatly and is assessed according to entirely different criteria.

The Standard may call for a specific size, weight, color, markings and other features depending on the breed. Only a fraction of the one million-plus dogs registered annually in the United States have serious show potential, and many of those never see the inside of a showring throughout their lives.

Even animals with an aristocratic background may be what experienced dog fanciers refer to as "nice pets" or "companion dogs." However, being a good pet or companion dog is as honorable a calling as that of the most exalted champion. The classification is not a condemnation of the dog itself. What it does mean is that such a dog falls short of the acceptable Standard of physical perfection required to compete successfully at AKC dog shows.

Beauty, in the final analysis, is in the eye of the beholder, as the saying goes. Excluding a crippling disability, an otherwise healthy dog can have the ability to become a fine earthdog and a great companion, regardless of what may be perceived as cosmetic physical imperfections.

For those interested in buying a terrier or Dachshund puppy as a prospective earthdog, good conformation is desirable but not absolutely essential. Prospective buyers should contact reputable breeders—people of integrity who are making an honest attempt to produce good dogs, preferably from stock with a working background. Most breed clubs compile lists of approved breeders and these are usually available for the asking.

MAKING THE RIGHT CHOICE

Folklore regarding the best way to choose the so-called pick-of-the-litter involves a great deal of mystic criteria. While making no guarantees, I've found that a good time to make one's choice is when puppies are from six to eight weeks of age.

A puppy's relationship to its mother, favorable or otherwise, can make a significant difference in its behavioral development in later life.

At this stage, puppies somewhat resemble what they will look like as adults; there is no way to accurately predict how good or bad a youngster will be when it matures. Some get better, some get worse. One can only separate the possible from the unlikely.

At twelve weeks, puppies start going through various awkward growing stages, much like human adolescents. For a time after that stage it is virtually impossible to seriously evaluate their true potential.

If possible, take a good long look at the parents of a puppy you may be considering, especially the dam. If the mother is a poor specimen, it's unlikely her puppies will be significantly better. The likelihood of a poor-quality dam producing high-quality puppies is decidedly remote.

Avoid puppies that are difficult to handle, or struggle or yelp when held. Choose one that, like these well-socialized youngsters, are accustomed to being handled.

Take mental note of the dam's behavior, how she treats her offspring, and how they react to her. How well the dam treats her puppies in the nest will help shape their temperaments later in life.

The sire is no more capable of working miracles, in terms of producing quality puppies, than is the dam. He can only contribute 50 percent of his future offspring's DNA, be it good bad or indifferent.

Regardless of the quality of the sire, a dam with a bad temperament, poor conformation or other faults, is certain to transmit similar blemishes to her offspring—genetically, if not otherwise.

If permitted to choose from several puppies in a litter, look for an active, alert youngster with a straight back, straight legs, good feet, adequate bone, and a bright shiny coat. There are some exceptions, however. If you are looking for a Bedlington or a Dandie Dinmont, bear in mind that both these breeds have properly curved toplines. Accordingly, a good Bedlington or Dandie puppy will show an indication of this desirable feature early on. On the same subject, Dachshunds and many of the low-stationed terriers will often show a slight east-west outward turn of the front foot below the wrist. This is completely normal and may become even more pronounced in the adult dog.

A puppy should be friendly, with a wagging tail and bright clear eyes. Young puppies should be carefree and uninhibited. Avoid quiet, shy individuals and any that yelp when handled in a normal fashion.

Above all, choose a puppy you can like. There is no knowing exactly how a dog will develop as it grows older. Pick one you can enjoy, warts and all!

Whether the puppy develops into a show dog or not is less important than its being a keen, alert, obedient, affectionate companion to share your life for the duration of its own life. Furthermore, there is no good reason why a dog of an otherwise qualified breed cannot be trained as an earthdog or participate in other organized recreational activities for which it may be eligible.

REGISTERING A PUPPY

Once a sale is finalized, you should receive either an official AKC registration application form or a registration certificate—completely filled out on the reverse side as indicated and signed over to you by the previous owner. This will enable you to transfer the dog's registration to your own name.

The AKC recommends that, if the seller does not give you the registration papers at the time of sale, you should request and receive valid identification of your dog, consisting of the breed, the registered name and number of your dog's sire and dam, and its date of birth. If the birth of the litter to which your puppy belongs has been recorded with the AKC, the litter registration number should suffice.

Don't be taken in by promises of "papers" later. Insist on a valid registration form or proper identification. If neither is available, pass on any puppy from that particular litter.

Only about one-half of the purebred dogs born each year are actually registered. The most probable reason eligible dogs are never registered is owner procrastination and losing or misplacing the required documents.

Once the litter or individual registration form is lost, there is little chance of registering a puppy without the cooperation of the breeder of record, not to mention a lot of red, white and blue tape! To avoid this problem, register your puppy immediately after you obtain its "papers."

For more details, one may request an informative pamphlet on the subject from the American Kennel Club, 5580 Centerview Drive, Raleigh, NC 27606.

Ch. Skaket's Candy Man, UDT, CG, TT

Ch. Dawn's Up N Adam, Am., Can. CDX, CG

Ch. Royal Scott's Lady Abigail, Am., Can. CD, CG

Ch. Dawn's Kop N' A PLea, **SE, CG**

Ch. Woodbriar William the Great, CD

Ch. Dawn's Kit N' Kaboodle, CD, **SE, CG**

Ch. Dawn's Shadow Dancin'

Anyone interested in buying a puppy for participation in Earthdog trials would do well to study the puppy's pedigree carefully. The presence of any ancestors with Earthdog titles (JE, ME, SE) or Certificates of Gameness (CG) in the pedigree is an important plus. The West Highland White Terrier, Ch. Dawn's Kop N' A Plea, SE, CG is a prime example of a proven Earthdog. She is also the dam of Dawn's Hole N' One, JE who shows successful Earthdogs in his sire's pedigree.

PUPPY TRAINING AND SOCIALIZATION

It is important to start training your puppy *to live with you* the moment he arrives in your home. There is an old saying that goes "each trainer will end up with the dog he or she deserves." That goes double for terriers and their owners.

PUPPY SOCIALIZATION

To a puppy, with its poorly developed visual system, children and adults may appear as two different species. Therefore, puppies must learn to accept both children and adults. "Love you, love your children" is not always part of the canine credo.

Meter readers and mailpersons may also look different to a puppy. It may be a good idea to introduce the youngster to each of these "species" during its initial socialization period.

Behavioral development varies within the critical socialization period. Testers evaluated the reactions of puppies ranging from five weeks, eight weeks, and twelve weeks old, confined to a room with one person equipped with a mild electrical shock device. All the puppies had previously experienced normal human contact.

The five-week old puppies actively approached the tester, but the majority ran away when shocked. When retested two weeks later, the puppies reapproached the tester.

It is important for us to realize how gigantic we appear to very small puppies and to behave accordingly around them. Do not swoop down and scoop a puppy up off the ground and hold it high in the air. Imagine how you, as a child, might have been traumatized by being picked up by an elephant and waved around or tossed up and down like a toy.

This reaction occurred because puppies are still very innocent when only five to seven weeks old. They will actively approach any animal species and freely socialize with that species, regardless of any previous emotional experience—good or bad.

The eight-week old puppy also actively approached the tester, but ran away when shocked. However, when retested two weeks later, this one refused to go near its tormentor.

The eighth week of life is the critical period of emotional development for the dog. A traumatic experience during this time may permanently impair the normal social instincts of a youngster. It is important to remember that the eighth week of life marks the beginning of stable learning.

Five- to seven-week-old puppies will freely interact both with their own kind and with other species. At eight weeks a puppy's attitude starts changing.

A well-socialized puppy that has reached age twelve weeks or older will stay close to humans, even if by doing so it incurs abuse.

Finally, the twelve-week-old puppy actively approached the tester. When shocked, it attempted to huddle as close to that person as possible. Its reaction illustrates an important phenomenon: A socialized dog feels safer when close to a human than it does by running away, and is willing to endure "punishment" to be with a person.

TRAINING PUPPIES

Shaping is a technique used to help train animals in certain disciplines; e.g., pushing down on a dog's hindquarters when training it to sit, as some trainers suggest.

Shaping, timing (e.g., taking the dog outside when it is ready to eliminate, in order to housetrain it), and immediate praise for performing the discipline being taught, are considered positive teaching and reinforcement techniques. Scolding and punishment are rarely effective ten seconds after an act, due to instant disassociation. As with all types of learning, motivation governs the success or failure of the lesson. For a social animal like the dog, praise is often more productive than fear.

Personally, I prefer the word "approval" to "praise." One is less effusive than the other. For example, effusive praise needlessly distracts from the accomplishment itself, whereas approval does not.

A couple of points need to be made about training a dog to be an enjoyable companion:

1) The animal must be in good health.
2) Commands, expectations, rewards, and punishments must be consistent and realistic. Inconsistency creates neurosis and mistrust.

Basic obedience training is valuable in teaching fundamental commands and in conditioning a puppy to the fact that humans, especially its family members, are dominant.

A puppy must be taught that it ranks lowest in the family social group, or hierarchy, and is not dominant to any member of the household, including any children. The annual statistics regarding the number of toddlers and small children bitten by their own family dog is much too high. The most probable cause: inadequate early socialization.

Wearing a Collar

Immediately put a small, lightweight leather or nylon collar on the puppy when you bring him home. Most puppies are too preoccupied with their new surroundings to notice the unfamiliar object around their neck. But, for very small puppies, a cat collar works quite nicely. The elasticized insert used in most cat collars is a safety feature that works as well for puppies as it does for cats.

Caution: It is dangerous to leave slip collars on dogs of any age. Slip collars should not be worn except during an actual training session and should be removed immediately after the training is finished.

Barrier Training

Barrier training is an easy way of restricting puppies and young adults to a selected area of the house, without making gates and barriers permanent and somewhat bothersome fixtures around the home.

There are various types of expandable, lightweight barriers available from local hardware or pet stores. Any one of these works equally well. But, choose one that is long enough to stretch across the opening you intend to obstruct, with several inches to spare.

This is the drill:

1) Set the barrier loosely in place.
2) Wait for the puppy (or young adult) to approach the barrier.
3) Before the dog gets too near the barrier, knock the barrier over with your foot—as subtly as possible. An alternate method is to tie a length of string to the top of the barrier, so you can make it fall down with a light

tug. Both methods work equally well. The intent is to startle the puppy—without hurting it. After a couple of near misses, most puppies develop an understandable avoidance response and stay well clear of that pesky gate. Once that happens, the gate becomes more of a psychological barrier rather than a physical one.

Take care not to injure the pup, accidentally or otherwise. For stubborn youngsters or young adults, repeat the procedure whenever the dog approaches the barrier. It's worth the effort. Occasionally it becomes something of an endurance contest. Most dogs will quit eventually, unless you quit first! And whenever you need to confine your dog to one particular part of the house, you can use the barrier with confidence, knowing he will not attempt to knock it down or jump or climb over it, as might occur with an untrained dog.

Leash Training

A simple nylon slip collar, often erroneously called and used as a choke collar, is the safest type of training restraint for most youngsters. However, a slip chain may be preferable for young adults and older dogs. It is virtually impossible for a dog to escape from a slip chain, and is safer to use than a regular collar when strolling along the sidewalk or in other public places.

Using a light nylon slip collar and a six-foot leash:

1) Carry the puppy—wearing its collar and leash—about one hundred yards or so from home.
2) Place him on the ground at your feet, holding the leash loosely in your right hand.
3) Give him a reassuring pat on the head and a few soft words of encouragement.
4) Start to walk briskly away as if you were leaving, with or without him.
5) Don't drag a puppy that doesn't follow. If you've bonded with your puppy it will soon become anxious at the

prospect of being left behind in unfamiliar surroundings and start to follow you.

6) If the puppy balks or hesitates, shake the leash or give it a light nudge or two, simultaneously encouraging the youngster to come to you. Be reassuring, never threatening.

Separation anxiety will make most puppies eager to stay close to their owners, especially if they have strong following attraction. All that is necessary is to lead them.

Let him explore this new world if he's so inclined. If he takes off in a different direction, follow him around a while, then ease him back on course.

7) Once the puppy follows happily, you can begin walking past your home for a short distance, eventually taking a stroll around the block or as far as you choose to go.

8) Keep him walking to heel on your left side as instructed elsewhere—if you can. However, at this stage, following you with confidence is more important than what side he's on.

9) Puppies should learn to follow their trainers up and down steps, through gates and small openings, and in and out of cars. It helps to alleviate their fear of these places in later life.

10) Puppies have brief attention spans. Keep lessons short and crisp—not more than four or five minutes long. Work with your puppy every day, until he follows to your satisfaction.

Don't wait to start leash training your puppy. If he is old enough to walk, he is old enough to train. However, do not take him to a place where he might be exposed to contagious diseases unless he has received his puppy shots and has sufficient immunity. Finally, in most cases, it is best to stay well clear of parks, vacant lots and open areas frequented by strays and unsupervised dogs.

Housetraining

Housetraining a puppy should be relatively simple. Generally speaking, it is only a matter of reinforcing a dog's natural reluctance to foul its living space. Given the chance, most puppies are predisposed to clean habits; few will willingly foul their nest if given an alternative.

Even so, the ease with which individual puppies can be housetrained varies, depending on their age and previous living environment. Puppies from a clean home environment tend to be much easier to housetrain than those previously housed in cramped, confined, or unsanitary surroundings. On the other hand, puppies deprived of the opportunity to develop clean habits may have already developed undesirable traits from a lack of alternatives. Unfortunately, the tendency is not easy to reverse.

It is important to understand that puppy training starts from day one. Obviously, the urgency associated with early housetraining is in direct proportion to the size of the dog. One can be more tolerant with small puppies than with young adults and grown dogs that can drastically transform the ambiance of one's home with recurring "accidents."

New owners tend to share the widely held misconception that the best housetraining procedure is to inhibit a puppy from defecating in the home. A better approach is to encourage him to relieve himself in a predesignated area or section of the yard. Same idea; different approach. Puppies should be exercised immediately following a meal or a nap.

One of the more common mistakes first-time owners make when trying to housetrain youngsters is to periodically dump them outside and leave them there, alone and unattended. This is a presumption that the puppy knows exactly what's expected of him, which is only wishful thinking. Early on, leaving a puppy alone in the yard tends to produce separation anxiety and little else.

A puppy may feel he's been evicted from his home and can easily forget all about nature's call. He may spend his "potty time" yapping and howling at the door, anxious to get back inside the house.

Once inside and feeling secure, he'll probably remember he needed to relieve himself and do so in the house—making his owner very unhappy. Scolding him, even immediately, can be counter-productive.

People tend to rationalize about animal behavior. Blame Walt Disney for our national anthropomorphism. One hears comments like: "He knows he's done wrong 'cause he hides under the couch when I enter the room." You bet he does! He knows his owner goes ballistic whenever he relieves himself indoors.

The fearful anticipation of angry outbursts may inhibit a dog from voiding while the owner's around. This is most significant if the dog is being exercised on a leash. Even after walking several blocks, a puppy may not relieve himself until he returns home and his owner exits the room.

To facilitate housetraining, it's best not to give a puppy the free run of the house. Confine him to one or two rooms where he can be under frequent supervision and quickly shuffled outside when necessary. Learn to read his body language. If he starts circling the room with a concerned expression on his face, it's time!

Owners should stay with the puppy and encourage him to relieve himself on command. Make up a code word. I use, "quick, quick!" It may sound a tad juvenile, but if it works, who cares? My grandson's six-week-old Jack Russell Terrier was 90 percent housetrained in less than a week using the prompt response system.

Outdoor training is always preferable. However, for very young puppies paper-training may be an acceptable alternative—especially during the winter or for apartment dwellers.

1) Start by spreading several sheets of newspaper on the floor near the puppy's bed.

2) Apply a drop or two of housetraining aid to the center of each page. Housetraining aid is available from most pet counters; however, a scrap of paper towel previously used to mop up a puppy puddle works just fine. When puppies feel the need to relieve themselves they tend to gravitate to a previously "marked" area—a pre-approved location.

3) Try to catch the youngster just before the act and encourage him with the code word or phrase of your choice.

4) A prompt response should be accompanied by a few words of praise as positive reinforcement. I am not an advocate of voluminous praise or bribery, but some trainers are. Whatever works for you is fine by me.

5) Once the desired response has been established, scent only one page of newspaper.

6) Gradually ease the scented sheet toward the door, systematically reducing the number of pages until only one remains.

7) Put the marked sheet outside, in the area of your choice, and encourage the puppy to use it. Stay with him until "it" happens. Housetraining takes patience.

8) After a couple of days discard the newspaper altogether. Apply a few drops of scent to the ground instead, and encourage the puppy to use that area. Stay there until he does so.

9) Praise him and take him back inside immediately. This teaches him that being prompt is the quickest way to get back inside the house.

10) Never leave a small puppy alone in the yard or exercise pen during the initial training.

NOTE: The above procedure works equally well, if not better, using two or three square feet of indoor/outdoor carpet. The carpet can be reduced in size, and/ or taken outside and left there permanently. The only drawback is having to hose it down occasionally.

Larger puppies should go outside from the start, no matter what. It helps to have a fenced-in area. A few drops of scent applied to the selected spot should help get things started.

Stay with the dog until he relieves himself. Praise him to show your approval, then take him back inside the house.

For those forced to exercise their puppy on a leash, the drill is much the same. Apply scent to the alley or the gutter, and walk him around until he takes care of business, then praise him and return home.

Responsible owners do not allow their dogs to foul lawns, public places, and parks in particular. Obey local ordinances and clean up after your dog. Even when not mandated by law it's mandated by good manners.

Crate Training

Crate training is essential for anyone planing to travel with a dog, whether it's to visit the veterinarian or groomer, or going on vacation, to a dog show, to an Earthdog Test or anywhere else. A dog is safer when crated than when jumping around in a fast-moving vehicle.

In addition, he will feel more at home when taken to a strange environment like a motel or a friend or relative's home. You won't have to worry about him settling in or doing any damage.

Contrary to how some owners may feel about confining their dog to a crate, most dogs like having their own private den (crate) where they can go to relax in peace.

Start confining the puppy to his crate for a short period every day, ideally after he's been playing and is ready to nap. Initially he may cry briefly, but if ignored he will soon stop. Your puppy should quickly become accustomed to his crate to your mutual benefit.

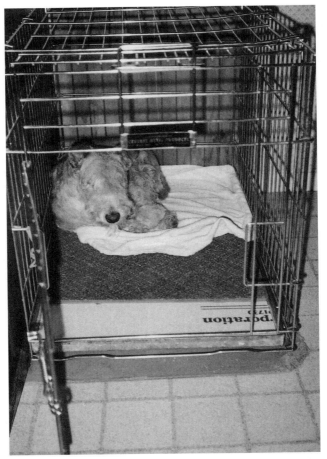

Contrary to the opinions of some owners, the great majority of dogs enjoy having their own space in the form of a crate.

Some trainers suggest that feeding a puppy in its crate helps develop positive association with crating. I'm ambivalent about it myself. Puppies that become accustomed to being fed when crated may object to being crated without also being fed.

Once a puppy feels secure in his crate, you can put the crate in your motor vehicle. Leave the crate in place a little longer every day for a week or so, depending on how quickly he adjusts. Make sure your vehicle is well ventilated and parked in the shade.

Terriers attending den trials are safest when confined to their crates when not actually in competition. They should also be crated enroute to and from the trial for their own and the driver's safety. There is a wide variety of crates on the market to suit any need.

Puppies raised in the home, as part of a family, are by no means precluded from becoming highly efficient earthdogs.

Once the puppy knows the routine, you can start taking short spins around the block to accustom him to riding in a moving vehicle. Progressive conditioning will make your terrier or Dachshund into a seasoned traveler in no time at all.

Some dogs enjoy riding, others don't. Not much can be done about that. Those that dislike riding must to learn to tolerate it. It's just that simple.

RAISING A HEALTHY PUPPY

Once your new puppy arrives home, it should be started on a strict feeding and training schedule. In most cases, no immediate food changes should be made. New owners are advised to use, within reason, the same diet and general feeding schedule the breeder did. However, there is no need to cater to eccentric breeders who choose to feed their dogs exotic home-cooked diets.

A great deal depends on the puppy's age, its previous environment and numerous other variables. One cannot anticipate every contingency.

It is recommended that all newly acquired dogs, young and old, be checked by a veterinarian for overall condition as early as possible. The new owners may get some real surprises.

As an example, my grandson and his wife know a great deal about high-tech computers and little about low-tech dogs. In good faith, they bought a Jack Russell Terrier puppy that the breeder claimed was six weeks old. After visiting the vet, they learned that in reality it was maybe four weeks old and barely weaned. As a curious aside, she is the only surviving recipient of a professionally administered puppy shot from a batch of contaminated vaccine.

FOODS AND FEEDING TECHNIQUES

Dogs and their owners today are very fortunate with respect to the wide variety, high quality, and ready availability of modern dog foods. Dry, canned and frozen foods are established staples at supermarkets and pet food chains everywhere, while veterinarians routinely furnish semi-solid puppy food and special formulations for dogs having particular dietary needs.

For newly-weaned puppies, a small amount of bitch's milk substitute, evaporated milk, or water added to canned food and mashed with a fork to a creamy consistency makes it easier for them to swallow. Canned, evaporated milk is usually okay. But cow's milk straight from the container is not as good because some pups, like humans, are lactose intolerant.

Human "baby" and "junior" foods made with beef are expensive, but will work on a short-term basis for small or very young puppies. However, they are too costly to be practical.

Because home-made bitch's milk substitutes may lack certain essential nutrients, multi-vitamin drops should be added to both regular and evaporated milk according to label directions.

Puppies from six to eight weeks old may require four or five small meals daily, although not all puppies will eat that much. If your puppy has been getting five meals daily, continue the same schedule. If he shows that he needs fewer meals during a twenty-four hour period adjust accordingly. Be flexible and understand that this is only a rough guide. The best source of advice on feeding your budding earthdog is your veterinarian.

After reaching eight to twelve weeks of age, puppies can gradually be switched to the diet you choose. Because puppies tend to swallow their food without chewing it, dry food should be moistened until soft but not mushy. Food that's too sloppy may cause diarrhea.

As puppies grow older, their food can be given dry, straight out of the package. Milk or milk substitutes can be discontinued at the owner's discretion.

The total daily food intake varies with individuals. Older puppies may benefit by having two meals a day. Most adults do just fine on one meal a day. The are no absolutes and owners are advised to experiment to determine what works best.

Although fresh drinking water should be available at all times, some puppies tend to drink too much at once. Others delight in wading in their water bowl and splashing around in it.

If your dog falls into either category, consider the following:

1) Weighted drinking bowls are available.
2) Small drinks of water can be given regularly between meals as needed and the bowls removed.
3) For a number of puppies, a two-gallon poultry waterer is a good way of controlling the amount of drinking water available at any one time.

As previously stated, puppies can be weaned by starting them on mushy food at about three to four weeks old, while they are still nursing. It is good to remember that the dam may choose not to clean up after her young once they start being supplemented.

For very young puppies, mash up a small amount of canned food in a shallow pan, with slightly more milk substitute or water than previously suggested. Dip each puppy's nose in the goo and wait. The majority will lick the mixture off their own nose or each other's, enjoy the taste, and look for more.

Some quickly learn to lap, others need a little more help before they catch on. Puppies will get themselves thoroughly "gooed up" and will need to be sponged down after every meal. Be sure to towel them dry and keep them out of cold drafts until they are completely dry, or they may catch cold.

Good eating habits are developed early by being consistent. Always feed at the same time(s) and at the same location. If possible, the same person should feed them every day. This helps establish mealtime anticipation that stimulates good appetites.

The dogs I feed come looking for me at mealtimes; those my wife feeds pester her. My dogs show up at the office door at four o'clock sharp every day, just in case the clock on the office wall has stopped working.

Dogs eat more in the winter, when it's cold, and less in the summer heat—especially outside dogs. That's to be expected.

Other factors aside, puppies that gain weight, look healthy, and act fit and lively are probably being fed appropriately. Bad doers—puppies that do not thrive—inactive, or lackluster youngsters with no apparent health problems may benefit from a change of diet. Some may benefit even more from increased attention and additional exercise.

For working dogs of all breeds, including earthdog prospects, a prerequisite for optimum performance is good health, vitality, and a great rapport with their owners and handlers. A happy dog is a healthy dog, or vice versa.

KEEPING YOUR EARTHDOG FIT AND HEALTHY

Diet and exercise play a significant part in keeping dogs fit and healthy. The foundation for good conditioning is a well-balanced diet, regulated to meet a dog's changing requirements as it progresses from puppyhood through all the stages of its life.

Nutrition has two parts: 1) Diet—the food the dog eats. 2) Digestion and metabolism—how efficiently the dog can utilize that food.

A good diet contains all the essential elements that can be utilized effectively by the animal: a complete well-balanced diet. There are many proprietary brands of dog food from which to choose. Some may be better suited to your dog than others.

Excluding vitamin C, all mammals require roughly the same vitamins and minerals. Most mammals, except man, produce their own vitamin C.

Dogs and humans alike require the correct balance of carbohydrates, fats, and proteins. A meat-only diet would be as inappropriate for a dog as it would for you or me.

Because humans have learned to enjoy a variety of foods, our diets require a great deal of planning and balancing. Raised correctly from birth, dogs are not as finicky; a balanced canine diet is infinitely easier to prepare.

Usually, adding table scraps and other forms of people food to titillate a dog's appetite could upset the nutritional balance of commercial dog foods. Dogs whose diets have been adulterated may gain or lose weight accordingly or show other signs of a feeding imbalance.

As they grow older, some dogs may require special diets; e.g., dogs with heart ailments may benefit from a low-sodium diet. Other specialized diets are formulated for kidney or liver disorders, food-related allergies, intestinal problems, obesity, and other problems.

Your veterinarian is the person best qualified to recommend the appropriate prescription diet, fully prepared and ready to feed to an aging or ailing dog.

Because some products contain more filler than others, diet digestibility is also a factor that needs consideration. A dog may require larger servings of a high fiber diet to satisfy his energy needs. This, in turn, may result in greater excretion, indicating not all the food was fully utilized.

Owners may also wish to consider the needs of their household when selecting from the three basic types of food available: canned, semimoist, and dry.

Canned foods contain a lot of water, but are easy to use and store and may be practical for smaller breeds. Open cans should be refrigerated to prevent spoilage.

Cheap canned food is likely to have low nutritional content. Always check the list of ingredients on the label. Look for words like "complete" and "balanced." At least one protein source (beef, lamb, chicken, meat by-products, etc.) should be included among the first three ingredients. A balanced diet should also contain cereal grain (corn, wheat, rice or oats).

Semimoist foods are somewhat less expensive than canned, but are generally loaded with salt and preservatives. These are a convenient choice where refrigerator space is limited. However, recent scientific studies tend to indicate that excessive salt intake may induce abnormally aggressive behavior in wild animals. The studies did not include dogs, but who knows?

Dry foods are cheapest and easiest to feed and store. Owners are well advised to use dry dog food before trying the others.

Having selected a brand that meets the necessary requirements, try it for a week or two. Weigh the dog before and after the trial run. A puppy should gain weight during this period; a mature dog's weight should remain stable.

Commercial dog food company advertising relies heavily on owner-appeal. Ads tend to imply a positive similarity between their product(s) and the food we eat—beef, hamburger, etc. But that "good-red-meat" appearance may be the result of chemical additives used to enhance eye appeal.

Convenience has always been a strong selling point for commercial dog food. Unless one is willing to accept a certain amount of inconvenience in feeding and in other aspects of dog care, perhaps he or she is best served by not owning a dog at all!

An important advance in canine nutrition was the introduction of the specialized diets. These nutritionally balanced diets are formulated to be used from the vital growth period of puppyhood (from weaning until maturity) to old age and all stages in between. This includes concentrated, palatable diets for nursing mothers, fortified with the extra calories and nutrients needed during gestation and lactation; a highly digestible, biologically efficient diet that requires minimum intake for healthy adult dogs maintained under normal conditions; and a high-energy stress diet to meet the added nutritional demands of highly stressed sick or working dogs. "Highly stressed" may include earthdogs, hunting and show dogs, dogs recuperating from surgery, and nursing mothers.

OTHER FEEDING REQUIREMENTS

In addition to an unspecified amount of carbohydrates, dog food should contain a minimum of 15 percent fat, 20 percent protein, and the correct balance of the following vitamins and minerals essential for maintaining a normal, healthy animal:

Vitamins: A, B, D, E, K, B12, thiamine, riboflavin, pyridoxine, pantothenic acid, niacin, choline, and ascorbic acid.

Minerals: calcium, phosphorous, iron, copper, potassium, iodine, magnesium, sodium, chlorine, manganese, cobalt, and zinc.

Based on experience, I suggest that a good percentage of young dogs may be undernourished in relation to their energy output. This does not necessarily mean underfed, though that may also be true. Conversely, older dogs are frequently overfed and consequently overweight.

As dogs grow older and less active their nutritional needs decline. Diets for aging dogs are formulated accordingly.

Individual nutritional requirements vary, along with the amount of food intake required for optimum good health. Extreme cold, increased activity, or physiological stress may boost "normal" requirements by as much as 200 percent.

Puppies from six to twelve months old (or until mature) may require feedings each morning and evening. Some do, some don't. The larger, slow-maturing breeds may need two meals a day for up to two years. However, that hardly includes terriers.

There are good doers and bad doers. The best yardstick is the growth, health, and vitality of the individual dog.

Dogs and puppies should be allowed 15 to 20 minutes to consume their meal. After that time the food should be removed. If the entire meal has not been eaten during that time, the amount of food should be reduced by approximately the uneaten amount, and the quantity increased as the dog's appetite increases.

If a dog is a poor eater—perhaps because its eating habits were poorly developed as a puppy—canned dog food may be the only food the dog will accept. Therefore, it becomes the only recourse for the dog feeder.

More often than not, a blend of dry and canned food will do the trick. Remember that too much mixing and blending may unbalance an otherwise balanced diet. With dogs there are no absolutes, trial and error is part of the game.

Semimoist and combination products that may contain excessive amounts of sugar, salt, and preservatives have dubious merit but remain popular with some owners. That in itself is not a crime; it's a matter of choice. Whatever works, works.

The task of selecting a balanced diet became easier once stricter regulations for pet food labeling were introduced. Manufacturers are now required to provide positive proof that their product is what they claim it to be and does what they claim it will do, nutritionally and otherwise.

Finally, do not alter a dog's diet without good reason. Dogs do not appreciate frequent dietary changes. Generally speaking, they prefer the same old chow every day and are better off in the diet department when you leave well enough alone. The many "taste tempting" flavors now available may well be major contributors to increasing numbers of fussy eaters.

In contrast, canned foods would require the addition of 100 percent fat to obtain similar results. This is a result of the high moisture (water) content, that is sometimes as high as 70 percent.

Note: Doubling the fat content of dry dog food reduces the daily intake requirements about ten percent. Increases beyond that may limit food intake and create a diet imbalance—a common problem when table scraps are added to commercial diets.

NUTRITIONAL SUPPLEMENTS

Although dog food manufacturers like to claim their products provide "complete nutrition" that does not need supplementation, the need for certain vitamins and minerals has been shown to skyrocket dramatically under stress situations.

Stress occurs following surgery or sickness; and during the growing and teething stages; pregnancy; lactation; periods of increased physical activity; and adverse weather conditions.

This suggests a need to supplement, intermittently at least. And this most certainly applies to poor eaters. An impressive analysis on a package is meaningless unless the dog ingests the contents.

Most dry dog foods are high in carbohydrates but low in fat, possibly to reduce the potential for spoilage. Adding certain oils or bacon fat could correct this deficiency. Daily amounts of fat should range from one teaspoonful for small puppies to one or two tablespoonfuls for active adults. Dietary fat yields the most energy and helps produce a good coat and healthy skin.

Experiments indicate that dogs consuming adequate fat are less excitable and likely to have better temperaments than those on low-fat diets. As might be expected, opinions vary greatly within the scientific community.

Vitamin A is essential for good eyesight and healthy skin. It is also required for the absorption of fat. Dandruff is one possible sign of vitamin A deficiency. Other indications include swollen joints, low fertility rate, and decreased levels of immunity to disease.

Vitamin B complex is essential for combating anemia; which, among other causes, may result from severe parasitic infections. Excessive hair loss, skin fungus, dermatitis and itching, nervousness, constipation, weight loss, listlessness, conjunctivitis, corneal opacity, and poor appetite are symptomatic of vitamin B deficiency.

Another indication of vitamin B deficiency is constant scratching and chewing of the feet. Brewer's yeast and liver extracts provide readily available sources of B vitamins.

Vitamin C is normally synthesized by dogs; therefore, ascorbic acid deficiency is rarely a problem.

Vitamin D is required in correct ratio to calcium and phosphorus for the development of strong, healthy teeth and bones. Lack of vitamin D results in rickets and other complications. Adequate levels of vitamin D are most important during lactation. Fish liver oils and natural sunlight provide vitamin D.

Vitamin E is essential for the muscles and internal organs to function properly and also contributes to a healthy coat and skin.

Vitamin K helps maintain normal blood clotting levels and is available from fish meal, liver, and leafy green plants. Vitamin K is synthesized by most animals. Excessive bleeding may indicate a lack of vitamin K.

Protein and Calcium, as a rule, are present in commercial dog food products in the form of ground bone. This also provides phosphorous, copper, zinc, potassium, manganese, magnesium, iron, and iodine. Both fish and meat are excellent sources of protein.

If infection or disease has been ruled out, a high mortality rate among newborns may indicate insufficient protein in the dam's diet.

The interrelationship between vitamins and minerals in the metabolic process is still not clearly identified. There is little doubt that a significant imbalance will produce undesirable and sometimes irreversible consequences. However, excessive supplementation also produces unfavorable side effects. The most frequently mentioned side effects are bone malformation and hip dysplasia.

TIPS ON FEEDING

Feed on a regular daily schedule. Regularity helps develop and maintain a healthy appetite and helps when house-training puppies.

Don't feed immediately after hard exercise or play, when a dog is hot and tired. Conversely, don't feed immediately prior to heavy activity, long car rides or airplane trips.

When trying to switch their dog's diet, some owners tend to become discouraged when the dog refuses to accept the new diet. The trick is to make the change-over in easy stages.

Dogs are creatures of habit. The best way to introduce a new diet is to start adding a couple of tablespoons of the new food to the old, while reducing the present diet by equal amounts. Over a period of a week or two, reduce the one and increase the other in equal amounts until the switch is complete.

For a diet to work efficiently, dogs must be free of debilitating internal and external parasites. Fleas, ticks, heartworm, whipworm, hookworm, tapeworm, roundworm and others occur all over the United States and Canada. The dog feeder must be ever vigilant against them and their effects.

Periodic worm checks by your local veterinarian are a must. If needed, he or she can then prescribe the appropriate treatment if and when worms are shown to be present. Indiscriminate worming is not advisable under any circumstances.

CONTROLLED EXERCISE

For most adult dogs, walking is the best form of controlled exercise. Walking improves muscle tone, tightens up the feet, hardens the pads, and wears down the nails. Walk your dog several blocks every day for a month or two and I guarantee you'll both look and feel better.

Chasing a ball or favorite toy around the yard for ten or fifteen minutes a day is better than nothing. Remember that dogs, like humans, should start exercising in moderation until they gradually build up their stamina and endurance.

HEALTH CARE NEEDS FOR OLDER DOGS

Just as human diseases associated with aging start appearing around age 40, canine problems are apt to show up at age six or seven—although we have a hardy thirteen-year-old Whippet that has never known a sick day in her life.

Older dogs become susceptible to liver and kidney diseases, digestive and skin ailments, food-related allergies, heart problems, and obesity.

Any of the following could be symptomatic of existing or impending health problems: excessive drinking, frequent urination, repeated stomach upset, listlessness, irritability, lameness, poor appetite, weight loss, and a chronic, hacking cough.

Regular preventative health care and a daily ration of kindness and affection can make an important contribution to an aging dog's continued good health and add years to its life. With sensible geriatric care, there is no valid reason why a canine companion's declining years cannot continue to be a happy, productive, and rewarding time for both dog and owner.

"What are you kids doing in there?" A concerned mother keeping a sharp eye on her pups playing inside a large cardboard box.

Puppies learn from experience. In the absence of a den, romping around inside an empty cardboard box can be a positive learning experience for them as they feel their instincts kick in.

There's one in every group! This bold little guy appears to be too adventurous for his own good.

PUPPY AND NOVICE EARTHDOG TRAINING

Given the chance, most terrier and Dachshund puppies are inquisitive enough to instinctively explore small tunnels, excavations, tight spots, and dark corners without encouragement.

The easiest way to encourage tunneling at an early age is to install a play tunnel between two adjacent exercise pens or runs. A tunnel easily closed off when necessary is the most convenient. A few nine-inch drainage tiles will make an indestructible tunnel that will last a lifetime and then some.

Put the puppies in one pen and their food in the other and you have instant tunnel training. In the unlikely event that there is hesitation, put one of the puppies in the pen with the food and the rest will soon join him.

A nine-inch pipe is big enough for six- to eight-week-old puppies of all earthdog breeds. As the puppies grow, the hole may become a little snug for some, but they'll continue using it at will, much like they would a pophole or doggie door.

Where space is limited, a puppy play tunnel placed against the wall or fence of the exercise yard is the next best thing.

Anyone with the space and the inclination can expand the tunnel periodically, maybe adding a right-angle bend in the process. It depends on how enthusiastic and determined one is to produce a topnotch earthdog.

Contrary to some beliefs, dogs may be claustrophobic, while others may experience barrier psychosis. It is wise to proceed slowly and with caution. And to some dogs, performing specific disciplines on command may prove to be less attractive than doing so spontaneously.

It is extremely unlikely that puppies accustomed to scrambling in and out of tunnels from the day they were weaned, or sooner, will ever develop an aversion to going to ground. Doing so quickly becomes second nature to preconditioned youngsters.

Some individuals clearly enjoy burrowing and tunneling more than others. Those who have known the misery of owning an "escape artist," or a dog that habitually burrows its way under the fence, know only too well how persistent these dogs are once they get started.

Because my wife is somewhat opposed to dogs rearranging her vegetable garden, I discourage digging. Anyone inclined to do so can start his or her dog digging by partially blocking one end of the tunnel with loose sand or soil in gradually increasing amounts. It's good to remember that sand is easier to brush out of a dog's coat than dirt and is not as messy.

For dogs slow to catch on, blocking off their retreat leaves them with no alternative but to go forward. Leave a glimmer of daylight to show them the way out. Be sure to reward that first effort.

Every dog trainer on earth develops his or her own quirks and training preferences. Although the mechanics may vary, the objectives are the same: namely, to cultivate a dog's desire to perform a given discipline consistently upon command; e.g., go to ground and work the quarry.

Partially blocking the ends of the play tunnel with sand is one way of forcing dogs to dig their way in and out.

Personally, I don't much care for dogs that perform like robotic automatons. I've seen some that remind me of battery-operated toys more than anything else. They amble to the end of the tunnel and stand there yapping at the quarry in a dreary monotone. They may pass the test, but they lack the fire and animation essential to true den dogs.

I believe earthdog training is best done in two stages:

1) Tunnel training.
2) Quarry awareness training.

The two may or may not be taught concurrently, depending on the age and temperament of the candidate. I have seen too many owners forcibly stuffing bewildered youngsters down a hole, assuming the dogs' "natural" instincts will automatically crank into gear and propel them to the far end

117

of a long dark, unfamiliar tunnel, where some unknown quarry lurks in wait. This version of forced training has been known to work, but it's not the best way to develop a good earthdog by any stretch of the imagination.

One reads and hears a great deal about certain breeds' "natural instincts." However, when these instincts have not been utilized for several generations it may take time and some encouragement to get them back up to speed.

Recent scientific research into genetic influence on so-called inherent behavior revealed all kinds of interesting data. Behavioral scientists now believe that calmness and wildness are each controlled by a single dominant gene. It's become trendy to attribute just about every facet of human and animal behavior, and general well-being, to previously undiscovered genes or DNA.

Call me a skeptic. Sooner or later most studies manage to contradict each another. What was true yesterday is false today and vice versa. Credibility is fast slipping down the tubes! Over the years I've noticed that rowdy or nervous dogs will adversely influence calm, quiet dogs to a much greater extent than the other way around. Don't put a good dog with a bad one unless you need two bad dogs!

It has been shown that cross-fostered pups, raised with a dam or litter of another breed, tend to retain certain inherited behavior patterns characteristic of their own breed regardless of how they were reared. Strangely enough, the individual rather than the shared experiences are the ones that shape character. It has also been well demonstrated that behavioral differences between individuals of the same breed will vary according to external influences: experiences, environment, exposure, isolation, general management, and the man in the moon.

Actors frequently employ a process they call "effective memory" to help them evoke certain emotions. The trick is utilizing any or all of one's senses to recall earlier life experiences—even those possibly suppressed in the subconscious. In theory, allowing that emotion back into conscious memory permits the actor to portray an entire spectrum of emotions in a more realistic and convincing way than might otherwise be possible.

I suggest that dogs and most other animal species use their effective memory to survive. There's no need to dig as deep as humans. An animal's effective memory, linked to all its senses, remains near the surface, geared up and ready to go. It is a virtual reference library of past experiences, good and bad alike, that influences an individual's actions or reactions to any given situation.

According to researchers: "Personality and temperamental features of a dog are shaped not only by genetic potential but also by the sum total of all [the individual's] experiences encountered during [its] development." The foregoing is simply a long-winded way to describe effective memory.

Perceptual or observational learning is also extremely important to young animals. My grandmother was annoyingly fond of saying, "Monkey see, monkey do!" whenever I did something out of line—which was often. Although more applicable to dogs than humans or hypothetical primates, grandma was more or less right on the money. Her view of perceptual learning had purely negative connotations. Whereas animals, perhaps more than humans, readily assimilate good and bad habits with equal ease.

A puppy's best (or worst) teacher is either its mother or a trained older companion. It learns behavior by watching and imitating the other.

Perceptual learning's biggest drawback is the fact that undesirable traits are as readily learned as the more desirable ones; e.g., incessant barking. Even so, in the majority of cases perceptual learning and earthdog training are extremely compatible.

TRAINING WITH LIVE QUARRY

The AKC rules governing Earthdog Tests stipulate that the live quarry will be two laboratory rats. From my experience, tame rats soon become too lazy or too placid to generate much excitement, unless a dog is naturally adrenalized at the mere sight of rats. However, not all dogs are affected this way.

The normal instincts of predatory animals, dogs included, are generally aroused by the quarry's attempts to flee. Blasé, hand-tame rats that ignore would-be aggressors to the point of taking a nap in their would-be pursuers' presence, are just too bland to excite some dogs.

It is important to know that rats, especially hungry rats, are most active at night. There may be a clue there somewhere!

Getting Started

Initially, I prefer to arouse a dog's curiosity and interest in the quarry's unfamiliar scent before resorting to visual stimulation. About 25 percent of a dog's brain is devoted to its applicatory senses and the specific task of identifying and analyzing the myriad scents that a dog normally encounters.

Smell is the dog's primary *effective memory* sense. This is a virtual olfactory encyclopedia that humans are not privileged to share. Smell is too often overlooked as a source of clues to many of our dogs' behaviors and responses.

All dogs remember and identify innumerable scents and odors with ease. A dog can detect the sent of one drop of vanilla diluted 1,000 times.

However, overpowering odors may temporarily reduce a dog's scenting ability to practically zero. Sniffing strong chemicals, such as gasoline, can dull a dog's olfactory senses for 24 to 48 hours or longer.

As a first step, applying a hint of rat scent inside the play tunnel will arouse immediate curiosity. What is it? Where is it? Curious, active minds want to know! Immediately!

Dogs instinctively gravitate toward unfamiliar odors. A strategically placed drop or two of diluted rat scent rarely fails to arouse curiosity, especially in familiar surroundings.

Use a simulated scent, which is available from sporting goods supply houses or by mail. Dilute it and use it sparingly; a drop or two is ample.

For step two, put a light application of scent in a remote corner of the yard. Having once discovered the scent, most dogs will almost certainly gravitate to that same spot at every opportunity; always searching, never finding.

I use commercial muskrat scent, when I can find it. If not, soiled newspaper or bedding material from the bottom of a rat cage works equally well. Lightly soak the bedding then drain off the water.

After several days, preferably after dark, several active rats or other rodents can be hidden near the area that was scented previously. The rats should remain well hidden and inaccessible to the dog(s).

Inaccessibility is essential in order to adrenalize the dog and get him fired up and eager to go. Let the dog find and attempt to reach the rats. He may not be able to see them, but his nose will tell him where they are. I've found this is an effective way to start dogs barking at the quarry.

After a few minutes, pick up the dog, praise him, return him to the house or kennel and remove the rats. Repeat this process a couple times without showing the rats to the dog. If he barks, praise him and demonstrate your approval.

Dogs must learn to use their noses as well as their eyes. Once they've developed good scenting habits the rest is easy. Young dogs may become keener working with an older, fired up brace-mate or hunting companion. Two youngsters rarely work as well together. This, however, is not an absolute. Level of performance often depends on the dogs and without an alternative, trying two young dogs together is definitely worth a shot.

Be careful when working with two dogs. When two or more feisty terriers with megadoses of adrenaline surfing through their systems get together with no alternative outlet, they may decide to expend some of that pent-up energy and excitement on each another. Fur could easily fly.

The next step is to place the rats within view and almost within reach of the dog(s), but not quite. Allow the dog(s) to work the quarry for approximately five minutes or less, to maintain their enthusiasm.

Remember the old axiom: "A little more than a little is by much too much!" This must be a variation of today's "less is more," I suppose. Either way, it should be part of every dog trainer's credo, to avoid overdoing any part of the training

Laboratory rats used as quarry can be sluggish and uncooperative at times. An earthdog's ability to qualify at any level is contingent on his keenness to work the quarry. It becomes harder when the rats don't help. Then it is up to the handler to arouse the dog's interest in these rodents.

regimen, whether training a dog to den work or for any other discipline.

The final step is to place the rat cage at the end of a short chute where the dog can see, smell, and all but grab the quarry. Include an artificial rat on the end of a length of string that can be manipulated up and down to help get the dog excited should the live rat(s) fail to cooperate.

Everyone has to work out his or her own method of isolating the quarry and limiting access to it via the chute. This will be governed by one's setup, ingenuity, and other variables.

In most cases, a regular eight-by-four sheet of plywood or the side of a large cardboard box with a hole cut out of it so it fits over the end of the chute (blocking off the dog's view of

A faux rat. One of the biggest advantages of faux rats is their dependability. Unlike the real thing, they are absolutely guaranteed to perform on cue—every time! *Kohler*

As the faux rat pops in and out of its hiding place, this youngster starts becoming adrenalized; his attitude is quickly transformed from curiosity to animosity. *Kohler*

Using a battery-driven mechanical toy, like this "Weazelball™," that rolls erratically in every direction, helps keep earthdogs interested in faux quarry.

the rats), works about as well as anything else. The idea is to thwart trainees from reaching the quarry except via the tunnel or chute.

Artificial Quarry

The greatest advantages to using artificial lures or faux quarry is convenience and low maintenance. A facsimile of a rat is easy to make and even easier to keep.

You will need a couple of feet of two by four, a heavy rubber band or a lightweight return spring, a length of cord, a couple of screw hooks, a piece of cardboard, a wooden dowel, real or artificial fur, rat scent, an anchoring device and a little ingenuity. Put them all together and *bingo*, you can make a simple, inexpensive artificial lure.

It is necessary to have a spare, unattached dummy rat to use as a reward and to generate further interest. There must always be a reward to stimulate incentive in the dogs.

Training a dog to react enthusiastically to fake quarry is a snap. More accurately, it's a combination of two processes.

It is preferable but not essential that the dog first learn to retrieve on command. Throwing a favorite toy around the yard and encouraging the dog to fetch and return it is a good way to start.

The second part of the process has unlimited options. Most dogs and puppies have a favorite tug-toy or something they like to worry and/or hang onto if someone is willing to hold onto the other end.

The trainer should engage in occasional but brief tugs-of-war allowing the puppy to always win. The process is similar to early schutzhund or attack dog training. The idea, as it applies to earthdogs, is to develop or increase a dog's confidence in its ability to secure possession of the quarry (toy).

The intensity of the contest should vary slightly each time. It is essential that the trainer quits before the dog does, but the dog must earn the victory. This greatly intensifies overall tenacity.

Retrieving is an excellent motivator. This lively Lakeland can hardly wait for the dummy to be thrown. Direct interaction between dog and handler is an excellent way to develop the rapport that must exist between a successful earthdog and its handler. *Kohler*

Sometime during this process, the trainee must learn the difference between the tug-of-war game and retrieving to hand. This becomes important as the training progresses.

One way to do it is by playing "fetch" in the house a few minutes every day using the dog's favorite toy. Soon it becomes a regular routine. It is something one must learn to live with.

Using different objects helps the dog to differentiate between retrieving and tug-of-war. Eventually he must learn to surrender the tug-toy, or anything else, promptly upon command. (Necessary obedience disciplines are outlined in Chapter 11, "Obedience Training for Earthdogs.") Finally, always give the dog enough time to "kill" his catch!

A terrier leaving a den having retrieved an object left there for that purpose. This is yet another useful ploy to avert boredom. *Kohler*

Go! Fetch! Find! Rats!

Assuming the disciplines outlined so far have been adequately mastered, it's time to introduce the dog to the artificial lure.

As always, the quarry must be placed slightly out of reach. I prefer a restraining barrier with horizontal bars that allows the dog to reach through with its forepaws and *almost* touch the lure.

The quarry should remain hidden, then pulled into view, cautiously, tantalizingly, mimicking the timorous actions of a jittery rodent. Meanwhile, encourage the dog to bark with whatever key command best suits your fancy. The idea is to generate as much excitement from your dog as possible.

To be effective the artificial lure must mimic the real thing, much like the lures used in spinning or fly fishing. Immediately when the lure attracts the dog's attention, let it pop back into hiding. Do the cat and mouse imitation several times, until the trainee is truly adrenalized.

Partially blocking the exit with a movable object, like a board, adds something new and prepares the dog to deal with future obstacles and constrictions it will encounter within the den as it proceeds in proficiency from one level to the next. Consequently, negotiating a constriction or obstruction within the tunnel should present no problem for the average terrier or Dachshund. *Kohler*

Then, with the lure once again concealed, toss the scented dummy rat a short distance away, simultaneously using your key command while indicating it landed. One command is as good as another, as long as it works.

If the dog reacts correctly; e.g., pounces on the lure and shakes it and/or tears it to bits, great! Let him have his fun. Don't try to save the lure from being destroyed. It's the cost of doing business and a good reason not to get too fancy with your equipment.

If the dog doesn't react this way, then pick up the lure and throw it again, using identical commands an gestures. Should the dog seem to lack interest, don't be discouraged. Tease him with the lure by vigorously shaking it under his nose, or swatting him lightly on the nose while making growling noises. In this game you do whatever it takes to generate sufficient interest and enthusiasm to help the dog get the job done.

When he grabs hold, as most reasonable earthdog candidates eventually will, shake the lure lightly as if it were a tug-toy, then release it immediately. A trainer must build up the dog's enthusiasm and excitement with words of praise and encouragement. If the tug-of-war game was taught successfully, it should be easy to expand upon. Remember that the dog always wins.

Determining the frequency of using the artificial pop-out rat is a judgment call. Discard it as soon as possible.

Once the dog is eager to play with and retrieve the dummy rat, it's time to combine this response with running the short chute.

Youngsters should learn to run the straight chute first, then to make one turn. It depends on how precocious they are.

Lure awareness and den work can be taught simultaneously, without combining them until the time seems right. This is also a judgment call.

A piece of corrugated cardboard stapled to the end of the liner makes an ideal "hazard" for younger puppies. Knowing they can push their way out of the hole with ease builds up their confidence and keeps them going forward instead of backing up and possibly leaving the den. *Kohler*

Depending on the individual, the two stages should come together almost spontaneously. It's essential that one follow the other as smoothly as possible. No trauma is involved. It may take awhile, but think of it as fun.

When all else fails, one might consider using the method suggested in Jacques du Fouilloux' *La Venerie* [Hunting] c. 1560, translated into English from the French by George Turberville in 1575:

> And whin you have taken the old Foxes and Bagerds [badgers], and there is nothing left in the earth but the young cubbes, take them to your Terryers and encourage them, crying, "To him, to him, to him": and if they take any young cubbe lette them take theyre pleasure

Consistently winning tug-of-war games develops a dog's tenacity and self-confidence to a remarkably high degree. However, the dog must also learn to relinquish his trophy willingly upon command; otherwise, he may become overly possessive and uncontrollably headstrong.

Got it; kill it! Having wrestled the prize away from their handlers, most terriers will give it a thorough shaking to ensure its demise.

of him, and kill him within the grounde. Beware that the earth fall not downe upon them and smother them.

That done, take all the rest of the cubbes and Bagerd pigges home with you and frie theyre livers and their blood with cheese and some of theyre own greace [grease] and thereof make your Terryers a rewarde. Shewing them always the heads and skynnes [skins] to encourage them.

Then again, maybe not.

11

oBEDiENCE TRAiNiNG FOR EARTHDoGS

Although not necessarily in accordance with my personal views on the subject, there are numerous books on basic obedience available to those interested in training their dogs. These cover just about everything, from teaching dogs basic good manners to competitive obedience. Some are better than others but, in general, there's little difference between them.

Unfortunately, most of the books on dog training are targeted at the owners of the reputedly more trainable working and herding breeds with a "one size fits all" approach. The remainder advise the reader on how to best correct or avoid behaviors that may occur as the result of previous bad management and/or ill-conceived training or lack of it in the first place.

If there's a common thread between these books, it's the notion that earthdog breeds are not ideal obedience candidates. That is perfectly understandable, but I've known excellent Doberman trainers who didn't adapt well to training German Shepherds and vice versa. It may have something to do with personal preference, breed prejudice, and other related issues. One thing is probably certain, few of these experts have spent much of their time training terriers to be obedient.

Although earthdogs need not be models of exemplary behavior, they must be under control. Disruptive behavior can and will get dogs excused from participating in den tests, and rightly so.

Simple, non-competitive obedience training offers a means to communicate with one's dog in a specific way. Basic disciplines need not be as well executed as one would expect to see at obedience trials. It is neither expected nor required. But good manners are expected.

With no prior training, obedience or otherwise, one dog's first dig may be a disappointing flop, while another's may work out fine. There's no knowing. It's always a crapshoot. However, there's a greater probability that, in most cases, even a partially trained dog will out-perform its untrained counterpart.

How to best train an earthdog is something of a trick question. As a professional I trained dogs of all kinds in assorted disciplines, from police dogs to lap dogs. Frankly, when it comes to obedience work, terriers do not match up well against breeds with proven obedience track records. There's no reason to expect otherwise.

Terriers, like other breeds, have their own established core personality traits. Within these somewhat wide parameters are individual characteristics: introverted, extroverted, passive, dominant, submissive, aggressive, or what may pass as brain-dead. Characteristics and temperament that separate individuals within a given breed influence whether or not some dogs will choose to please their owners or themselves.

To use a very broad analogy, it is highly unlikely that a world-class tennis player could outrun a world-class marathon runner, or that the marathon runner would beat the tennis player at his own game. However, there's nothing to prevent a runner from playing a respectable game of tennis, or a tennis player from running a marathon. The same

principle applies to dogs; the key to perceived success or failure lies in realistic expectations.

I believe that dogs in general and terriers in particular are
best trained at a leisurely pace. I apply a somewhat simplistic
philosophy to dog training; namely, if a dog executes a given
discipline correctly one hundred times consecutively that dog
is trained. It works for me.

The debatable issue is whether or not the feat should be
accomplished in a day, a week, a month, or a year. If a dog
consistently responds correctly, training time becomes a non-
issue. Contrary to conventional wisdom perhaps, I discarded
highly repetitious training methods many years ago. For dogs
with brief attention spans, constant repetition tends to be
counterproductive. It gets old fast.

Eager workers are the best workers, although not necessarily the most polished. I would take genuine enthusiasm
over robotics precision every time.

The value of repetitive training diminishes as the grind
goes on. Continually repeating successfully performed exercises is an invitation to failure.

Much like flipping a coin; there is a 50-50 chance it will
land either heads or tails. The odds never change. The laws of
probability may come into play and effect the outcome, but
the odds remain constant, honest! How does this concept
relate to dog training? It's simple. Each time a dog is required
to perform an exercise there's an equal chance of success or
failure. On the other hand, an exercise attempted once and
performed correctly equates to a 100 percent success rate. My
motto is "quit while you're ahead." It's a hard sell, but it
works.

Older dogs and young adults may come loaded down
with old baggage—a plethora of built-in or acquired idiosyn-
crasies or traits that need to be modified, eliminated or
replaced.

It is imperative that neophyte trainers learn to identify behavioral tendencies and adapt the training accordingly. Initially at least, it is equally important to know what to correct and what to ignore. The success of counter-conditioning is usually governed by the age and temperament of the dog.

Overnight transformation is unlikely to occur, so don't expect or demand perfection. Let trivial things slide; concentrate on what's important. The rest will come later.

As most owners know, terriers respond best to easy progression. Generally speaking, they are more easily led than driven. A heavy-handed approach can easily ruin a good prospect.

Earthdog trainers should not rely on a dog's presumed latent or "natural" instincts, including its desire to go to ground. Many so-called natural instincts are acquired through social interaction and perceptual learning. A puppy's early environment and previous interactions with humans and other animals play a significant part in shaping its temperament and character in later life.

Puppies deprived of social learning may display aggressive, timid, obstinate, or unruly tendencies. A trainer must learn to roll with the punches and work with what's there. Never take a dog's actions personally. The secret is to always remain detached and objective, no matter what the dog does.

For a puppy's natural instincts to develop fully, it must serve its "apprenticeship" with a teacher or teachers of its own kind. Puppies learn from the dam's example. This could entail keeping an entire litter with her for an extended period, allowing the pups to watch and learn as she goes about her daily routine. For the most part, that no longer happens. Sad to say, that method of schooling has become obsolete and impractical due to current dog-rearing practices.

Breeders are compelled to interfere with, or interrupt the ongoing process of perceptual learning, as might normally occur in the wild, when puppies are between six to twelve weeks old—during the most critical learning and socialization stage of their lives. Most young dogs are wary of the unknown. Therefore, a prospective earthdog may need motivation to enter and exit the confines of a strange den on command. Training can accomplish that.

Most terrier breeds are naturally vocal, but in today's world one needs a workable compromise between nuisance barking and den barking while working quarry. Training can also accomplish that.

Teaching dogs to bark only after they locate the quarry is not always easy. Consequently, some terriers may become noticeably more vocal in the home following den training. That may not please everyone. One solution is to train dogs to quit vocalizing upon command—a way to have your cake and eat it, too.

IMPORTANT RULES TO REMEMBER

1) Exercise your dog before each lesson. Give him enough time to relieve himself, but do not initiate play prior to a training session. Dogs should not confuse training time with playing time, although they should enjoy both.

2) Try not to generate needless excitement. A calm, relaxed attitude helps establish the correct teacher-pupil relationship. Enthusiasm is altogether different from excitement.

3) Some individuals have short attention spans. The length of a training session should not exceed a dog's attention span. Ten minutes or less is usually enough. A couple of lessons daily, several hours apart, lasting approximately only five to six minutes may work even better.

4) Start each lesson with an easy exercise. It gets you off on the right foot and provides an immediate opportunity to show approval.

5) Develop a firm, crisp, authoritative word of command. Make each command clear-cut and final. Do not bully or coax your dog. A casual command produces a casual response. A threatening command produces an uncertain or timid response and sometimes no response at all.

6) Never allow your dog to disregard even one single command. Having given a command, make sure it's obeyed. Do not give a command you can't enforce. If you allow your dog to disregard or ignore a single command, you can be sure it will do so repeatedly. The idea is to convince the dog that disobeying a command is undesirable, if not impossible.

7) Never permit yourself to become agitated or impatient during training. Training requires time and patience. Impulsive behavior on the trainer's part may destroy a dog's confidence in him. Corrections must be *made immediately and indirectly.* "Indirectly" means using an impersonal approach that disassociates the trainer with whatever negative reinforcement is being applied. Scolding would be personal, whereas a jerk of the leash applied without malice would be impersonal.

8) Never permit a dog to become passive or to assume a defensive or submissive posture; it may develop into an alternative form of disobedience. Use reassurance instead of intimidation. Don't take no for an answer, but be a good guy, not a bully or a tyrant.

9) Use your dog's name as a cue before a moving exercise; e.g., "Spot . . . heel!" or, "Spot . . . come!" Use only the relevant command for inactive or stationary exercises: "Sit!"; "Down!"; "Stay!"

10) Maintain an emphatic tone without appearing to sound threatening or hostile.

11) Take a brief training pause following each exercise. Make the dog sit attentively (preferably to heel) while you remain motionless, doing absolutely nothing. It is important that dogs learn to be quietly attentive and

under control. Training pauses should comprise approximately one-third of each training session.

12) THINK TRAINED! More often than not, anticipating an appropriate response produces the required response. Maybe it's telepathy or perhaps it helps eliminate uncertainty in your own demeanor. Either way, much of the time it works wonders.

   The secret of successful dog training, if there is one, is staying relaxed and natural. Don't get worked up when the dog does well, or out-of-shape when he does badly. *Being uptight doesn't hack it,* especially with terriers.

13) Don't court failure. If a lesson is not getting through, switch to something easier before a bad attitude develops. Don't paint yourself and your dog into a corner. You can always return to the previous exercise later.

14) End each and every training session on a positive note. Allow the dog to *earn* your approval. Don't be afraid to fudge a little to make it happen.

15) Don't let other family members play at training the dog. One inexperienced trainer is sufficient for most canine trainees to handle at any one time.

HEEL!

All dogs should learn to walk quietly by an owner's left side without pulling or jerking at the leash or winding it around their owner's legs. Known as "walking to heel" or "heeling," it simply means the dog is walking quietly alongside the owner's left leg. This important aspect of a dog's schooling establishes control and sets the tone for all future training.

A well-trained dog will automatically assume the correct heeling position, on or off a leash, without needing a command. Frankly, that's not necessarily true of terriers!

Start the exercise with the dog standing or sitting at your left side, his shoulder approximately in line with your left leg (training Diagram 1).

Diagram 1. "Spot . . . heel!" Learning to walk at heel teaches a dog to adjust its pace to that of its handler, and walk beside him or her without pulling or tugging at the leash or lagging behind.

Hold the leash neatly folded in your right hand with your forearm approximately horizontal to the ground. Let the slack hang down in a loose loop as shown.

The leash should not be taut at any time during training, except when teaching the dog to "Stay." The actual amount of slack is governed by the size of the dog and the length of the leash, and controlled by raising or lowering the right arm.

Remember this rule: When moving forward with your dog, step off on your *left* foot (the one nearest the dog). The leg movement then acts as a cue.

As previously stated, the command "Heel!" is always preceded by the dog's name: "Spot (pause, two, three), Heel!" Using the dog's name acts as a "cue." A cue gets a dog's attention, allowing him added time to understand and respond to the command in a timely way.

A second visual cue is a sharp forward thrust of the open left hand with the palm turned towards the thigh. If at the same time you brush the side of your thigh with your hand, the sound it makes becomes a third cue.

This cue should immediately precede the forward motion of the left leg. Because most of us are accustomed to reciprocal motion—for example, right leg and left arm moving forward—getting the timing right may take practice.

Why two or three cues? Because verbal and visual cues are twice as effective when used together than when either one is used alone. Both should be used whenever possible. The more cues the better.

The first step must be taken in a positive, unhesitating manner. Take one, two, three steps and halt. Pause and wait.

SIT!

Before completing the final step and coming to a stop, give the command "Sssit!"—a long hiss followed by a crisp "T." The command can be accompanied by a slight sideways/upward motion of the right hand holding the leash; another cue. The arm motion should somewhat resemble that of a hitchhiker thumbing a ride. Immediately let the arm return to its original position, as if it were spring-loaded. At the same time, make a slow pendulum-like swing, or pass, over the dog's back, going from head to tail. Keep your arm close to your body when doing so.

The return pass should continue past your thigh. Allow the back of your hand to brush the side of the dog's head—if the dog's height allows. Hopefully, this will also encourage the dog to sit facing front when you come to a stop. However, as long as he sits, it really doesn't matter.

This maneuver also takes advantage of a dog's kinetic awareness—a sensory ability few humans possess and fewer yet will ever understand. Kinetic awareness may be the fabled *sixth sense* that enables dogs and other animals to "predict" earthquakes.

The command is "Sit!"; not "sit facing the front, or elsewhere." If the dog's butt hits the deck he's in compliance. Accept it and show your approval (Diagram 2).

Diagram 2. "Sit!" Whether on or off the lead, sit should mean "put your butt down on the deck," nothing more. Unless one plans to participate in competitive obedience, don't be too choosy; one "sit" is just as good as another.

Diagram 3. Should a dog decline to sit when told, a light upward pull on the leash (up and back) lifting his front feet barely off the ground, will ease him onto his haunches and into the required sitting position with no fuss or trauma.

If the dog fails to sit, grasp the leash with your left hand, about twelve inches from his neck, and ease his front feet a couple of inches off the ground. At the same time, ease him backwards onto his haunches (Diagram 3).

Repeat the command "Sit!" just once. Keep his front feet barely off the ground until he complies. Once he sits, immediately lower his feet gently to the ground and show your approval. The way to show your approval is with praise—a touch on the head and a few words telling him he did well, nothing more.

Immediately after he assumes the desired position, allow the leash to go slack. Repeat this exercise at each training session until the dog sits automatically whenever you stop walking. Going into an automatic sit is not a big deal, but it helps reduce fidgeting and anchors the dog in one place during the training pause.

Make it a point to be a little unpredictable in your training. Walk only a few paces before making the dog sit, instead of walking around the block. Stopping at random intervals, helps keep the dog's attention focused on you. Most dogs are less inclined to forge ahead to see what's happening around the next corner if they have something else to think about.

If your dog forges ahead when you start walking, make an abrupt about-turn each time he does so. This maneuver automatically puts the dog behind or alongside you again.

Repeat this as often as needed. Each time he draws up alongside your left leg, make him sit.

If the dog repeatedly surges ahead, yank him sideways and pull him off balance as you turn. Take it easy. No need to yank him too hard to get your point across.

Alternate between walking forward three or four steps, turning, halting, sitting, and pausing until he gets the message. If he lags behind, slap your thigh with your open hand and tell him to heel, just once.

When a dog fails to respond immediately don't take it personally. It is possible for dogs to get confused or downright ornery during early training. Act as if nothing unusual happened and start over.

Latent, or delayed action learning is not uncommon in dogs. Such a response is not willful. Faced with such a dog, rely on your patience, determination, and consistency to produce the training results you are seeking.

To attain the most rapid conditioning, the trainer should try putting together the longest unbroken streak of correctly performed exercises possible.

Contrary to some opinions, it is more effective to take a dog out, perform a single exercise correctly and quit, than to repeat the same exercise a dozen or more times with only a single mistake.

STAY!

As soon as you obtain a reasonably consistent response to the first two commands, add the "Stay" command to your repertoire.

Start with the dog standing or sitting to heel. Pull its collar up behind its ears with the slip-ring under the chin. (Note: For stationary exercises that require the handler to move without the dog, step off with the right foot instead of the left foot to avoid giving the dog the wrong cue.)

Hold the leash twelve to fifteen inches from the dog and bid him "Stay!"—just once. The best way to hold the leash for this exercise is over the flat, open palm of the hand, held there by thumb pressure.

Simultaneously with the stay command, bring the open palm of the right hand around as if you were going to slap the dog on the nose. DO NOT touch the dog, but try to make him blink. This is intended to distract the dog momentarily as you leave his side. Call this a negative or "non cue," for lack of a better term.

Immediately step across the front of the dog with your right foot (take one long stride) and, pivoting on the ball of the foot, swing your body around a full 180 degrees so you are facing the dog. Bring the left foot beside the right. At this point you and the dog should be standing face to face, directly in front of each other.

The maneuver may take some practice—unless you can waltz. It's a bastardized waltz step of sorts: stride, pivot, foot to the side, relax. Done correctly, the dog will remain sitting directly in front of you as you stand, feet slightly apart, holding the leash taut and slightly above his eye level.

As a preliminary exercise, try holding one end of a broom handle vertically in your left hand at arm's length. Using the same arm and leg movements as previously described, make a 180 degree turn around the broom handle without it moving. This will help you develop the correct muscle memory sequence needed for this discipline.

Learn your part of the drill correctly before attempting to teach the dog his. It's a team effort. Get it wrong and the dog will surely do likewise.

In theory, after you pivot, the palm of the right hand should remain extended a few inches from the dog's nose. That, however, does not work well with smaller breeds.

The next step is to reverse the process just described. Reverse pivot, returning back to where you started—standing beside the dog. Then show approval.

Repeat this exercise until the dog sits tight, showing no indication of breaking. A couple of days of drilling should suffice, at which time you can start backing slowly to the far end of the leash. Keep your left arm extended at shoulder height and the leash taut while stepping back.

Allow the leash to slide smoothly under your thumb as you back away from the dog (Diagram 4). Try not to jerk the leash. Maintaining constant but moderate tension on the leash will tend to make the dog lean back, anchoring itself in

Diagram 4. "Stay!" Using a taut leash to hold the dog in the desired position is an easy way to teach this discipline. It is important that a handler remain motionless and not inadvertently cause the dog to break with body language that may serve as a cue for the dog to move.

place. Jerk the leash and most untrained dogs are sure to break. Don't reprimand the dog, just start over.

Keep your right palm facing toward the dog, gesturing him to stay put if he appears unsteady. Wait only a few seconds before returning to his side. Read the dog's body language and minimize the chances of failure with good anticipation.

Finally, once the dog is steady enough, you can allow the leash to go slack, maybe resting on the ground as you return. Place your left hand on the dog's head, and after a brief word of praise, walk around him and return to the "heeling" position where the exercise began.

If necessary, leave your left hand on top of the dog's head a time or two to steady him. Some phases are easier to do than others, depending on the size of the dog, the height of the handler and other variables.

Don't push your luck. If the exercise works as intended, show approval and call it a day. Make it a "win-win" situation for all concerned.

SPOT, COME!

Successfully recalling a preoccupied terrier may never have been meant to happen. Frequently it doesn't! Having taught your dog to stay, teaching him the recall is a walk in the park—maybe.

Start the exercise as you would the "sit-stay" until you're standing at the far end of the leash facing the dog. At this point, bring your arm down, allowing the leash to hang in a slack loop, as opposed to keeping it taut as before (Diagram 5).

Now give the command "Spot . . . Come!" Pat your thigh and encourage him to come to you, at the same time bend at the knees, bouncing slightly. Your body language should

Diagram 5. "Spot . . . Come!" To encourage a dog that is in the stay position to come when called, merely slacken the leash and call to him by name. Use positive body language, like patting your thigh.

invite him to come toward you. Repeat the command a couple of times if necessary. In doing so, there is no need to raise your voice. A dog's hearing is up to forty times greater than ours, so shouting can achieve far more harm than good.

As the dog approaches, give the command "Sit!" before he actually reaches you; soon enough for him to understand and respond. When he gets to within an arm's length, reach out and grasp him lightly around the muzzle or under the chin and ease him into a sitting position directly in front of you. If he's slow to sit, repeat the command *once,* then raise his front feet off the ground while easing him backwards onto his haunches.

To get the dog back to the correct heeling position, first gather the leash in your right hand. Then, giving the command "Spot . . . Heel!" step back with your right foot while keeping most of your weight on the left foot, but allowing your body to sway backwards. There is no need to move far with a dog of a small breed. Simultaneously give the leash a brisk jerk towards the rear, transferring the leash from right to left hand—behind your back. This should be done in one continuous movement.

If the dog starts moving toward you, stepping forward with your right foot will put him slightly behind and to your right. Give the leash (now back in your *left* hand) a light jerk out and forward, guiding the dog around behind you. At the same time, return the leash to your right hand in front of your body.

Give the command "Spot . . . Heel!" take one or two steps and make the dog sit. By this time, the dog should automatically be sitting by your left side. If not, give him the appropriate command.

Changing the leash from one hand to the other is something of a juggling trick that takes practice. Look at it this way, in addition to training your dog, you are learning to waltz and juggle.

DOWN! . . . STAY!

The final exercise is the "Down" command. For most terriers it's an optional exercise. In some cases it can be more trouble to teach than it's worth. However, because it is a useful discipline, it is really up to the owner to decide whether to teach it or not.

The dog is required to lie down and stay down, until you command otherwise. The easiest way to teach this to a terrier is to kneel by its side and, grasping the leash close to the dog's neck with your left hand, give the command, "Down!" Meanwhile, pat the floor or ground with your right hand directly in front of the dog. This action is accompanied by short, light jerking motions on the leash (Diagram 6).

Diagram 6. "Down!" This exercise is not a terrier favorite but is easily taught by applying the right technique. Unlike the recall command, it's not used in Earthdog Tests. Whether or not you teach it is purely a matter of personal choice.

If the dog responds negatively to the jerking motion—and some terriers will—grasp its front legs with your right hand and, instead of patting the ground, draw the legs forward in front of the dog, tugging sharply sideways on the leash and pulling the dog onto its side. This will accomplish one of two

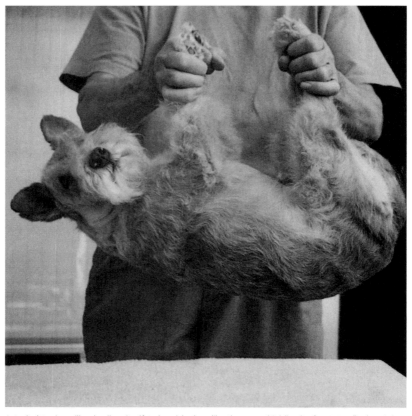

A typical terrier will only allow itself to be picked up like the proverbial "sack of potatoes" when it has complete confidence in its handler.

things: Either it will stretch him into the correct position and keep him there or pull him off balance and onto his side.

Once the dog is down, put your free hand on his side, using slight, downward pressure on his shoulder or chest with the left hand. Repeat the command "Down" followed by "Stay!" If he struggles to regain his feet, try to calm him down without undue commotion.

As a preliminary to this exercise, I teach my dogs to relax by lifting them up by their four legs like a sack of potatoes. It is easily done while sitting or resting on the couch. It is much like teaching dogs to tolerate grooming. Start when they're young and they soon grow accustomed to it.

Now walk to the end of the leash, as instructed for the "Stay" command discussed earlier. Then pause and return. If a dog appears unsteady at first, simply step on the end of the leash to ensure he won't take off for parts unknown (Diagram 7).

Diagram 7. "Down . . . Stay!" The down/stay is a very useful discipline. For the best results, never recall a dog from the down/stay. Given time he will come to understand that **you** will return to him; he need never come looking for you, even when you're out of sight.

Never call your dog to you from the "Down" position. He should learn that once he's down he's there to stay there until *you* return to him. He is never to come to you from the Down.

Don't over-praise your dog. Make him earn that approval. Remember to follow each exercise with a short *training pause.* This lasts a minute or more, during which time the trainer remains completely motionless while the dog sits (or stands) attentively at his side, *developing patience.*

Most neophytes view training solely as an "activity." Consequently, their dogs are not specifically trained to be purposefully inactive while quietly waiting for the next command, their turn to run, or whatever activity is being pursued. This is completely different to the "Stay!" exercise where the dog learns to remain in one spot until the trainer returns.

The Collar as a Communication Link

When you work a dog consistently, he soon learns to interpret the sounds made by his training collar. These sounds telegraph your messages as clearly as any spoken commands and affect his ability to respond promptly.

Unfortunately, a nylon collar fails to transmit messages in the same way. With a nylon collar one loses that additional, though perhaps not essential, means of communication.

The most sonic type of chain is the chrome-plated brass variety, which is expensive and hard to find these days. But, the nylon collar has its uses. It is great for training puppies, as previously described, and it won't wear away the hair around the neck of long-coated breeds if worn continually— which I do not recommend. However, it's not an equally efficient training device.

GLOBAL TRAINING

Using the global, or whole, training method which I prefer, dogs start learning all the required disciplines more or less immediately. Over a five-week training period and using the

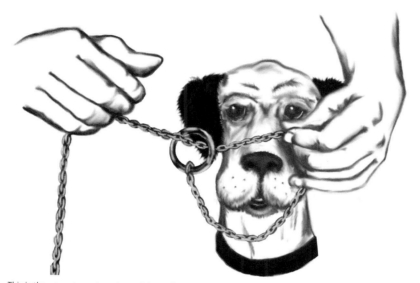

This is the correct way to put a training collar on a dog. If the "live" ring is not positioned as indicated, the circumference will not change and the collar would be useless for corrections. Slip collars should be removed as soon as training is concluded to prevent potential mishaps such as accidental choking.

traditional methods, a dog would have been learning one exercise a week. Whereas using the global method, the dog would have been learning all of its exercises simultaneously. With traditional methods a dog would have been learning to "heel" and "sit" for five weeks, to "stay" for four weeks, the "recall" for three weeks, and the "down and stay" for two weeks.

Contrary to traditional methods, when I trained dogs professionally, I conducted my lessons on a busy side road adjacent to the park opposite my kennel. There was a busy highway on one side and a railroad track on the other. If it sounds as though there were distractions galore, there were.

Although it is frequently recommended by trainers and writers alike that training be conducted in a quiet isolated area, I believe the more distractions the dog encounters during training, the better the outcome will be. If one starts by training a dog for several weeks in a secluded place, likely as not, as soon as the dog encounters unfamiliar distractions his mind will be elsewhere.

It seems better to get him acclimated to face the real world from day one. It doesn't make training more difficult. If anything, it makes it easier. Dogs tend to be less secure away from their natural environment and generally more accepting of the trainer's guidance and approval while in unfamiliar surroundings.

As most obedience classes are conducted by individuals who are or were involved in competitive obedience, far too much emphasis is placed on technique. For them, it is not sufficient for a dog to simply sit. He must sit perfectly straight, facing directly to the front at a specific distance from the handler, and reflect the kind of response sought in obedience trials.

Technique, per se, has nothing to do with sitting whatsoever. Given the command "Sit!" a dog should respond just as quickly as he knows how. Having done that, he has indeed "sat."

I suggest that hauling him into this or that precise position, a technique known as *shaping*, is unnecessary and needlessly confusing for a dog—especially a terrier.

Owners must establish in their own minds what constitutes being "trained." As indicated earlier, in my opinion, an animal that performs given disciplines 90 percent of the time or more is trained. If you put a dog through its repertoire correctly the first time, you have a 100 percent response rate and the training session is over.

Once a young dog is trained he won't automatically stay trained indefinitely. Dogs revert rapidly. Given the opportunity, most terriers develop bad habits much faster than they adopt good ones. Owners need to stay on top of the situation—it does keep terrier owners alert.

All breeds, especially terriers, must be kept in shape with regular tune-up training sessions until fully mature and beyond. Counter-conditioning to alter a dog's established responses to certain situations is another matter. If, when you attend your first Earthdog Test, your dog comes up short, don't give up hope. Identify the problem and seek a solution, maybe with the help of an expert.

Above all, never take out a failing performance on the dog. Abusing one's dog in that situation is not a solution, it's an admission of defeat.

ESTABLISHING A POSITIVE BARKING RESPONSE

For most dogs, learning can be instantaneous. A traumatic or unexpected experience associated with any activity may well deter a dog from performing that activity ever again. The term for that is "extinction."

Pavlov's experiments with dogs clearly demonstrated both *conditioned* and *unconditioned* responses and also *extinction*. Applying this knowledge to earthdog training is easy to do.

The act of a dog barking for food without any previous encouragement or other inducement would, in most cases, be regarded as an unconditioned response. Rewarding the dog with a treat in response to barking provides positive reinforcement, predictably resulting in more barking for food, which then becomes a conditioned response, e.g., "Speak for cookie!" Withholding further rewards or positive reinforcements for the act of vocalizing will eventually cause the dog to cease barking for food, resulting in the possible extinction of that trait.

Earthdog owners whose dogs decline to bark at rats have a definite problem that must be solved if they wish to be successful at trials. As judges cannot distinguish between conditioned and unconditioned barking, all we need to do is consult Doctor Pavlov.

Most dogs are quirky about something—excluding cats—that virtually drives them up the wall. That is where individual ingenuity comes into play. The owner either finds that trigger or invents one.

Because my wife and I tend to discourage random barking, our own dogs have never been particularly vocal. My Lakeland Rusty's reluctance to bark might have been a problem, had I not known his trigger was birdseed. Birdseed! Sure, why not birdseed?

For reasons unknown to me, whenever I filled the bird feeder this normally mild-mannered dog would go berserk, jumping, barking, snapping and generally going crazy. I've been nipped in the leg a few times in the process and a whack or two on the head with the lid from the plastic birdseed container didn't faze him one bit.

Inspired by this inexplicable behavior, I put a handful of birdseed in a coffee can and then shook the can vigorously when he reached the quarry. At first, the dog barked only when he heard the birdseed rattling in the coffee can, but with positive reinforcement, barking soon became a habit and the problem was solved. Thank you, Dr. Pavlov!

How well a gimmick works depends on the dog. When a friend's Dachshund proved equally mute in the den, I tape-recorded a couple of rowdy dogs barking and growling menacingly at each other. We played the tape good and loud when the dog reached the quarry; it worked like magic. Some dogs need a jump-start to get them going.

ESTABLISHING A POSITIVE RECALL RESPONSE

Will positive or negative conditioning make dogs come when called? You bet! Conditioning a dog to come when called 99.99 percent of the time is accomplished by what psychologists refer to in human psychology as "phobia indoctrination," perhaps better known as scare tactics.

Phobia indoctrination is nothing more drastic than negative reinforcement applied *before* instead of *after* an undesirable act occurs. You might say phobia indoctrination is psychological payment in advance.

That the idea may not appeal to everyone is a given. However, when I trained dogs professionally I would ask hesitant owners whether it was more humane to train a dog to obey or to have him destroyed. Everyone has choices to make. This is but one.

Negative conditioning requires nothing more than a simple throw chain and reasonably good interval timing. Interval timing is difficult to explain. Basically, it's the ability to identify that fraction of a second of reaction time between the thought and the deed.

The first requirement is a throw chain. I used discarded training collars. As you can see by the accompanying photo, my throw chain is fastened at each end and in the center with a small key ring to which is attached an old rabies tag.

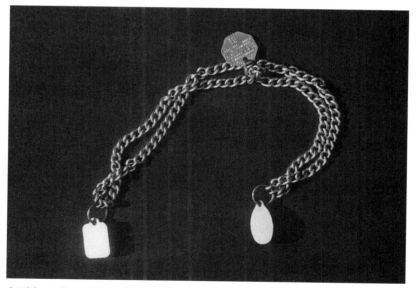

A training or throw chain as described in the text.

When the chain is tossed up and down in your hand it will make a distinctive jingling sound the dog will learn to recognize as well as he does your voice. For all intents and purposes it's your new voice; the voice of authority.

To condition the dog to come when called involves creating an insecurity (phobia indoctrination). This allows the trainer to be supportive and provide whatever security or reassurance the dog happens to need. Needs vary, especially with terriers. Surprisingly enough, you end up being the good guy.

Ideally, you should take the dog to an unfamiliar environment where dogs tend to be more responsive and dependent on their owners. Either that, or they will take off, never to be seen again. For that reason you'll need either a fenced area about the size of a tennis court or 20 to 30 feet of lightweight checkline attached to the dog's collar.

When you arrive at your destination, you must hold your conditioning chain tightly in your throwing hand, so it cannot jingle and alert the dog. Then, turn the dog loose and let him run. As soon as he gets ten to fifteen feet away, depending on whether he's running or walking, toss the chain firmly at his feet. Recall him the moment the chain hits the ground. Don't yell, use a strong, firm word of command that does imply a treat.

Some dogs will stop and sniff the chain, others may walk around it. Watch the body language for signs of uncertainty and then call again, but only once. If the dog does not come, turn around and walk away. If you get all the way to the end of the checkline give a sharp tug and call again.

When the dog comes to you, demonstrate approval with a touch on the head and make him sit. Reinforce the security represented by your presence by standing with the dog by your side for at least two minutes. This should help reassure him that nothing unpleasant will occur while he's with you. You become his safe haven.

If the dog is on a checkline, gather it in while you're waiting. After the appropriate pause, retrieve the chain as quietly as possible; keep it hidden in your hand or put it in your pocket. Repeat this exercise once or twice a day at different intervals until he gets the message.

A hard-headed dog may need the chain to connect firmly with his rear a time or two before he pays attention. However, the idea is to startle the dog without hurting him. Inflicting pain will totally negate the intent of the exercise.

After a couple of days, instead of throwing the chain simply jingle it in your hand before calling. The dog's response should be exactly the same. After a week or so, call without using the chain. Should he hesitate even a moment, jingle the chain immediately.

Indoctrinate the dog into believing he must come when called OR ELSE! If he is slow to catch on, keep working him until he gets it right. Work with your dog until you are confident of his response in any situation.

Throughout the training you will be positively reinforcing the recall merely by being there. Your reassurance and approval will be his reward.

"Here goes nothing!" A youngster's eagerness to enter a tunnel depends a great deal more on adequate preliminary training and confidence-building techniques than on innate instinct. *Kohler*

Look what I've found!" An excited puppy pounces eagerly on the "pretend rat" awaiting him at the end of a short chute. The dummy is tossed into place *after* the puppy enters the den from the opening at the opposite end. The next step is to replace the faux rat with either the real thing or one of several artificial, mechanically operated facsimiles, as indicated in Chapter 10. However, there is no need to rush the process during the early stages of training.

EARTHDOG TRAINING 102

As a rule, breeds required to perform specific disciplines are chosen for their predisposition and suitability to the required tasks. Generations of selective breeding have produced breeds with the appropriate physical makeup, innate instinct and a ready interest or willingness to perform a wide variety of functions. Den work is only one of many.

Although Bloodhounds and German Shepherd Dogs are the breeds of choice for tracking and trailing, dogs of any recognized breed are permitted to enter obedience and tracking trials held under AKC rules. As a matter of fact, individuals of some very unlikely breeds have been permitted to qualify for the highest working and tracking titles offered by the AKC. In contrast, Earthdog Tests are limited to Dachshunds and the previously specified den terrier breeds.

How best to train an earthdog will depend on its age, breed and general upbringing. Despite the fact that the eligible terrier breeds share a common background, at this point some seem decidedly more adaptable to den work than others. Putting it another way: by and large, certain breeds appear to have retained their hunting instincts better than others. That the best hunters do not always make the best pets or companions may have a great deal to do with that.

According to author Frederick W. Cousens (member of the Royal Society of Veterinary Surgeons, veterinarian to King George V and Edward VII, and dog show judge and head veterinarian to Crufts Dog Shows), "a listless terrier with the manner of a lapdog is an abomination."

For better or for worse, much of today's thinking on that score has changed. In the past, bolting or drawing dangerous quarry required a hard dog. That is not to say it should be wild and unmanageable, as some were, or have a bad temperament, as some did. Years ago, a working terrier had to be willing and able to stand his ground against whatever adversary it encountered, whether above ground or below.

Today we have individuals protesting the fact that conformation judges occasionally allow terriers to spar harmlessly in the show ring. Notwithstanding, sparring behavior is meant as an indicator of typical terrier temperament.

It should be obvious that in our society the need for truly hard terriers and Dachshunds has long passed, but to excel as an earthdog a candidate still needs a certain degree of toughness and determination.

A hard dog comes with a hard eye. There's a difference between hard and angry. The ability to distinguish between the two requires a good deal of experience.

The same may not be true of puppies. Puppies are difficult to evaluate. They may be unsure of themselves, and even timid in unfamiliar surroundings. A future "demon of the dens" may be a "shrinking violet" as a young puppy.

A trainer must know how to build up a dog's confidence slowly and methodically suppress undesirable characteristics while retaining its desirable predispositions. This must be done over a period of time; the duration depends on the dog. Of equal importance is the need to dispel any fears the dog may harbor, especially the fear of going to ground, should it exist.

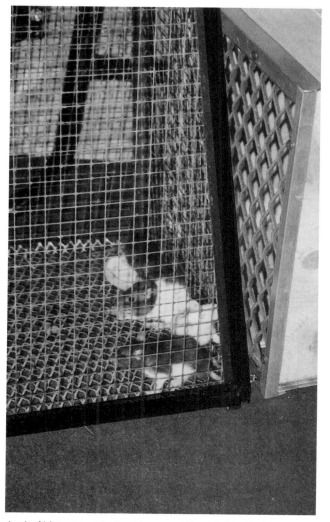

A pair of laboratory rats is placed in a cage at the end of the den liner to act as live quarry. At actual trials, the rats would remain hidden from sight in an underground den at the end of the liner. However, the cage is more easily photographed above ground. The rats are well protected and in no danger of injury.

Training an earthdog is similar in may ways to training attack and guard dogs—not the same, but similar. The key to successful training is knowing how to develop a dog's confidence slowly and progressively.

In one end and out the other. There's nothing complicated about that. A young Lakeland entering a short chute from the reverse end knowing a reward awaits him at the other. *Kohler*

In 1937, Elias Vail, then a noted professional trainer of sporting breeds shrewdly observed:

> The temperament of the individual to be trained, rather than the breed selected, can have a more decided influence on the progress made and on the speed with which we can advance from one step to another.

That has not changed in sixty years.

There are natural-born earthdogs, much as there are natural-born human athletes. However, expert training invariably enhances that ability and raises the performance levels of both species.

"Natural" confidence-building starts in the nest immediately after birth. The strongest puppy stakes its claim to the best teat, grows even bigger and stronger than its littermates and goes on from there. Will that make him the best earthdog prospect? Heck, no! Unfortunately, though, the best prospect may be ruined even before it leaves the nest. How a puppy is raised from birth will greatly influence his degree of gameness, or lack thereof.

Breeders should never allow one puppy to bully another, nor lose a skirmish with a bigger puppy or an older one. Weak puppies are easily intimidated and likely to develop temperament problems.

No matter whether the liner is short or long, a well-trained dog will go where the handler sends him. Terriers taught directional commands, similar to those used at retriever field trials, are generally more adaptable and rarely unfazed by any changes in their established routine. Using different commands for different exercises, even when disciplines are basically the same, helps dogs differentiate between somewhat similar exercises. One way to teach the "sendaway" is to seal off the primary entrance to the training den and direct the dog to what would normally be the exit. Directional exercises can be reinforced while practicing retrieving exercises by throwing the dummy where it cannot be easily seen. *Kohler*

Eager dogs can hardly wait for the fun to start. This Lakeland is exceptionally partial to coyote fur. It's a good idea to ensure a dog is adequately motivated prior to working on a particular discipline. *Kohler*

"Let's go, already!" No lack of motivation here. *Kohler*

One of my dogs was stung by a bee or wasp while still in the nest. From that day on he was spooked by flying insects, including house flies.

Confidence-building takes time and patience. "Dump him in at the deep end and watch him swim" is ill-advised philosophy.

Another important factor is whether or not a terrier or Dachshund is a kennel dog or a companion dog in its owner's house. It's one thing to have a testy dog outside or in a kennel and another to have one sharing your home.

Most of us would like the best of both worlds. Fat chance! The obvious answer is an acceptable compromise: a tolerable, pleasant companion blessed with sufficient hunting ability and the desire to get the job done.

This is what it's all about—an earthdog going to ground. *Kohler*

When he emerges from the tunnel, this Lakeland Terrier is rewarded for his good performance. His reward is finding the quarry. It's just that simple. The reward method being used, identical to that used by law-enforcement agencies to reward a find by "sniffer dogs," constitutes a positive reinforcement. The method works just as well for earthdog breeds as it does for drug-detection dogs. I do not use a barrier at the end of the tunnel during training, making the reward immediate. *Kohler*

167

Hunt terriers need no encouragement to go to ground. As graphic proof, Jill, the larger of the two Jack Russells shown here, tears away the sod with her teeth to widen the hole, while her smaller bracemate is able to dart under her legs and is first down the hole. According to their handlers, den dogs would stay in an earth all day if they were allowed to do so. Such intense desire cannot be taught; it can be cultivated, but only if it already exists. *Carlo Corby*

An earthdog's job is to locate the quarry's hiding place and verify whether or not the den is occupied before the handler starts digging. *Carlo Corby*

HUNT TERRIERS AT WORK

Hunt terriers or working terriers enjoy what they do. They need no encouragement to go to ground. Quite the reverse. As one handler remarked: "The little buggers'd be down there all day if we let 'em."

The only reason for sending a hunt terrier to ground is to locate the quarry and hold it at bay until the handlers can dig down to the objects of the search. To help their earthdogs do this more quickly and easily, today's terrier men use a homing device that attaches to a dog's collar and relays directional signals to a hand-held receiver "up top." The technology is new, but the idea is not.

In his renowned *De Canibus Britannicis* (1570), translated into English from the original Latin six years later by Abraham Fleming, Dr. John Caius wrote:

> **Of the Dogge Called Terrar, in Latine *Terrarius***
> Another sorte there is which hunteth the Foxe and the Badger or Greye onely, whom we call Terrars, because they (after the manner and custom of ferrets in searching for Connyes [rabbits]) creep into the grounde, and by that means make afrayde, nyppe, and byte the Foxe and Badger in such sort, that eyther they teare them in pieces with theyre teeth beyng in the bosome of the earth, or else hayl and pull them perforce out of their lurking angles, darke dongeons, and close caves

or at least through conceaved feare, drive them out of their hollow harbours in so much that they are compelled to prepare speedy flight, and being desirous of the next (albeit not safest) refuge, are otherwise taken and in-trapped with snares and nettes layde over the holes to the same purpose.

Is that poetic, or what!

In Volume II of *The Sportsman Dictionary* (1803) William Taplin wrote: "If the fox ran to ground, the huntsman, who was provided with good terriers, was to lay him up in the earth." Which, in the opinion of his contemporaries, "was sooner done by putting a collar of bells on the terrier's neck."

Another well-intentioned but misguided reason for using collars, some liberally adorned with sharp iron spikes, was to protect the terriers' necks against bites from their quarry. One might surmise that for a terrier trying to out-maneuver a fox or badger within the restricted confines of an underground den, the cumbersome neckwear was probably as hazardous to the dog as to its adversary.

A similar suggestion appears in *The Sportsman's Dictionary* (1735), stating:

> . . . your terrier must be garnished with bells hung in collars to make the fox bolt the sooner; besides the collars will be some small defense to the terriers.

In his uncompleted book, Welshman Sydenham Edwards (1805) agreed but offered a more practical reason for using bells:

> A small bell or giggle may be fastened to the collar of the dog, which will assist in alarming the fox and making him chamber sooner; and also direct those who dig with more certainty. So great is the terrier's perseverance, that some have been known to remain in the earth for days together, until fox and themselves

have been nearly starved to death. [Probably snagged by their collars!]

Before the advent of microchips, how quickly handlers could locate their charges varied with the terrain, the weather conditions and the type and size of the earth, all of which diffuse sound in different ways.

A dog that became fatigued and quit barking might well have been difficult to find. At times, locating a mute terrier trapped underground required much backbreaking spadework. In contrast, modern terrier men can pinpoint a dog's exact location and dig down to within inches of the quarry.

A small electronic homing device sometimes attached to an earthdog's collar, that sends signals back to a hand-held receiver, helps locate the dog after he goes to ground either in a large earth or in dense cover.

Contrary to what one might suppose, terrier men are not anxious to make their dogs become fearless fox fighters. This may have happened once-upon-a-time, perhaps, but no more.

For the average small terrier, challenging a mature adult fox that is backed up in its den is not a wise move. The slash and retreat attack of a cornered fox is difficult to elude unscathed. Wisely, today's terriers tend not to attack the fox.

Veteran terrier men try to discourage their charges from tangling with the foxes down a hole. They prefer keen, vocal terriers, able to find and work the quarry at a relatively safe distance, without putting themselves in serious jeopardy.

Chances that a dog might sustain a crippling, if not fatal, injury are all too real. A litter sister to Penny (one of the hunt terriers shown here) was generally regarded as too aggressive for her own good. As is often the case, this lack of discretionary valor proved to be fatal. A vicious dog fox literally ripped off her snout, necessitating euthanasia.

Digging their way down to the quarry, terriers have been known to block off their own retreat. Unable to advance or retreat, the safest approach is to settle in for an old-fashioned standoff and wait for help. Also, terrier handlers frequently prefer bitches to dogs because they are smaller and generally less aggressive.

During a hunt, a team of four terrier men will usually split into two pairs with one dog each. In the field it becomes extremely difficult for one man to juggle a brace of andrenalized terriers.

It is customary for two men to drive ahead, conveying the group's heavy digging equipment in a pick-up truck. The remaining pair follow the hunt on foot, walking and jogging and keeping up with the hunt as best they can, so that when a fox lays up they can move in and locate its whereabouts.

British law permits only two men to be present at a dig site. Once the fox is located, the terriers are removed from

The expensive "Ferret Finder" is buckled onto Penny, a Lakeland/Jack Russell hybrid, immediately before she enters the hole. Considered a safety device, it's the only collar a terrier wears when going to ground. *Carlo Corby*

Watched by her handler, Penny goes to ground. *Carlo Corby*

Once the dog disappears from sight the handler will listen intently at the entrance to the hole. If she bays, he will locate her exact position and dig down to the game, in this case a fox. When the quarry is found the terrier is removed and the fox shot with a humane killer (a powerful airpistol) and given to the huntsman. *Carlo Corby*

Jill, a battle-scarred veteran of numerous campaigns, has the experience and good sense to avoid a serious confrontation in an underground den. One of her littermates paid dearly for being too bold and aggressive. Terrier men are anxious to prevent incidents that result in the loss or mutilation of their dogs. *Carlo Corby*

Mission accomplished, but there's no fox there! A disheveled, disappointed Penny emerges from an abandoned den. *Carlo Corby*

the hole and given to one of the other handlers, who by law is required to stand back, together with the pack and huntsmen.

Having dug down to the fox or foxes, the man in charge at the hole reaches in, grabs each one by the scruff of the neck and shoots it at pointblank range with a "humane killer." A humane killer is a powerful airpistol which the bag man keeps hidden in his satchel—along with the directional collar and other miscellaneous essentials required for terrier work.

The fox carcass or carcasses are immediately given to the huntsman who throws them to the pack to reward the hounds.

Unfairly perhaps, biased television coverage of fox hunting often focuses primarily on this, one of the more grisly aspects of the hunt, with little or no elaboration. This kind of media exposure allows indignant viewers to assume the fox

The senior terrier man (left) gathers in the pack under the watchful eye of Bernard Parker, huntsman of the Mid-Devon Hunt, with whose gracious permission the photos in this chapter were taken. The hunt's whipper-in is in the center. *Carlo Corby*

The pack takes off down a long country lane, eager to "draw" or find the fox. This pack is comprised of a mixture of Welsh and Old English Hounds. There's a considerable contrast between these English Foxhounds and their American counterpart, whose development was impacted by a radically different set of hunting conditions. *Carlo Corby*

was thrown to the hounds and torn apart while it was still alive. The exact same sound bites are frequently aired on North American television.

By and large, foxes are treacherous, opportunistic predators wrapped in a deceptively-attractive, eye-pleasing, and sympathy-evoking package. While they may appeal to animal lovers, small farmers hold a very different view and for good reason.

Given the chance, a single fox will wantonly kill every fowl it can reach in a henhouse. A fox will do this, not for food, but for the sheer enjoyment it derives from the killing, or so it seems. I've seen the results of such a foray and it's not a pretty sight.

Two handlers, equipped with their dogs and the tools needed to unearth the fox, drive out ahead of the pack to the likely area of a dig. Based on previous experience, the terrier handlers will try to anticipate where the huntsmen will take the pack and hurry to get there first. Meanwhile, a second pair of handlers and dogs will follow the hunt on foot, jogging cross country behind the pack. *Carlo Corby*

Not all terrier men travel in style. This one, from a hunt in North Devon, accompanied by three Jack Russell Terriers, rides a pre–World War II bicycle, with fixed brakes and only one gear, to take him ahead of the pack. *Carlo Corby*

Getting to the Fox's den is sometimes easier said than done. This brace of terriers, eager to reach the quarry, unceremoniously drag their handler through the thick gorse undergrowth into a dense copse of trees where foxes are believed to be have taken refuge. *Carlo Corby*

In most cases, when hunt terriers are not sent to ground they are allowed to sniff the hole as a consolation prize. The leash stays on to prevent them from going down the hole and staying there for as long as they choose. *Carlo Corby*

Training terriers to confront a fox in the confined space of a subterranean lair is a gradual process. Serious training rarely starts before the terrier is 18 to 20 months old.

Initially, young terriers may be worked with seasoned brace-mates. Together they explore abandoned badger setts, frequently used by foxes. However, foxhunters discourage their dogs from chasing rabbits or going to ground in rabbit warrens unless there is good reason to believe a fox has been there also.

This is not done out of consideration for the rabbits. Rather, handlers don't want the terriers to develop a nose for rabbits when they should be focusing their attention on foxes.

Trainers tend to use deep, gruff voices and sharp commands delivered as close to the entrance to the warren as possible. (In certain circles, this could be construed as a form of "phobia indoctrination.") Even so, once the dogs are down a hole, their enthusiasm is such that obedience is not always the first priority. It's surprising how quickly young dogs learn from watching their elders (perceptual learning). This proves that my grandma's "see it, do it" theory was valid after all.

In the British Isles, depending on whether a hunt is located in an affluent or less-prosperous district, one or two terrier handlers may be kept on more-or-less permanent retainers, assisted by farmhands helping out on a voluntary or part-time basis in return for job-related fringe benefits or other perks.

Despite claims by the anti-hunt lobby that hunting dogs frequently attack domestic livestock, for which foxes were blamed, Jill goes about her task of the terrier's work seemingly oblivious to the herd of sheep grazing nearby. The sheep are similarly unfazed. *Carlo Corby*

There are no hard and fast rules of remuneration for this type of service. Terrier men may stay with one hunt their entire lives, or drift from one place to another as the spirit moves them.

Due to an abundant food supply and a significant reduction in hunting, foxes in the United Kingdom are thriving. Because foxes are more plentiful today than ever before and absolutely in no danger of extinction, the once mandatory "earth stoppers" have become redundant. However, as recently as 30 to 40 years ago, when hunts were many and foxes were few, an earth stopper would ride out prior to the commencement of a hunt and plug or stop up the abandoned badger setts and dens where foxes might otherwise take refuge.

The majority of earth stoppers were relatively insignificant individuals, performing their duties anonymously without fanfare or recognition. The singular exception was seventy-five-year-old Arthur Wentworth, earth stopper to the Earl of Carlisle, immortalized in the much reproduced engraving *The Earth Stopper* by John Scott, after a painting by Nathanial Drake. It has been suggested that reproductions of *The Earth Stopper*, first published in William Daniel's *Rural Sports* (1801), long ago surpassed all other terrier sports-related illustrations on the planet.

RATS!

Those who wish to train their earthdogs on live rats are welcome to do so. I decline to use them, except occasionally, only because I don't like rats and have nowhere to house them. I prefer an artificial facsimile which, manipulated correctly, works equally well if not better.

Should you choose to use live rats, use only captive-bred rather than wild specimens. Most pet stores sell such rats as a source of live food for large, exotic reptiles.

Pet and laboratory rats are derived from wild brown rats. Handled correctly, they can become very friendly and are quick learners.

Although generally friendlier than mice, rats will bite if provoked. For some reason, brown or colored rats seem less tolerant than the familiar white variety. When mishandled on a regular basis, both varieties quickly lose their trust in humans.

My brother Paul, a noted expert on racing pigeons, was also the rat and mouse king in our home. He once allowed a dozen or so white mice to escape. He recovered about half of them; the escapees interbred with uninvited house mice. Consequently, before you could say "whoops!" there was an abundance of pinto-colored rodents scurrying throughout our house, not to mention a couple of exceptionally contented cats.

Rats require feed and housing systems similar to those used for gerbils, hamsters and mice, but larger. They should be of adequate size, but not necessarily elaborate.

Some individuals may feel sorry for rats being kept for terrier work and training. Don't. They are not cognizant of their destiny and are not related to Mickey Mouse!

HEALTH PRECAUTIONS AROUND RATS

Before deciding to use live rats, keep in mind that they are also quite susceptible to respiratory disease. *Mycoplasma pulmonis* is a prime infective agent. It is also responsible for a chronic disease that occurs in almost all rats exposed to abnormal or unsuitable living conditions.

Caution: Even healthy rats normally carry the bacterium *Streptobacillus moniliformis* in their noses and throats. This organism can be transmitted to humans and is responsible for the disease commonly known as rat-bite fever. Another organism, *Spirillum minor,* occasionally found both in rats and mice, can also induce rat-bite fever in humans. Earthdog enthusiasts with small children should make note of that.

Where there's food there are rats. That's as true today as it ever was. Most of us choose not to dwell on this truth unless we must. However, in spite of greatly improved sanitation and food storage techniques and advances in vermin control measures, rats remain with us and are unlikely to disappear anytime soon.

History has failed miserably to record the rat's humongous, detrimental impact on the world economy. King of all vermin, rats eat, contaminate or destroy literally billions of dollars' worth of food and wreak many other kinds of havoc annually even in our own enlightened time.

Rats spread disease everywhere they go, and they go everywhere. Fleas from black rats were responsible for the spread of London's dreaded bubonic or black plague that in 1665 killed more than 110,000 people, or roughly a third of that city's inhabitants. More would have perished if the Great Fire of 1666 had not purged the city of literally millions of potential vectors.

A short time earlier, much of Europe had suffered a similar fate. One unfortunate event Nostradamus failed to predict was that his entire family would succumb to the plague in France while he was away ministering to victims of the disease elsewhere.

The disease is primarily transmitted to humans by infected fleas, but transmission by infected animals can also occur. Potential plague carriers include prairie dogs, rock squirrels, chipmunks, deer mice, field mice, pack rats, cottontail rabbits and tree squirrels.

Plague-carrying fleas can also exist on foxes, skunks, badgers, bobcats, coyotes and domestic pets visiting endemic areas. The important difference today is that, with timely diagnosis, the majority of cases are treatable with antibiotics.

However, in India a single outbreak of the deadly plague is believed to have claimed the lives of over 12 million people. In the slums of Bombay, where existing conditions may rival those of 16th-century Europe, municipal rat catchers continue to trap an estimated 4,000 rats each day, 365 days a year, year in and year out. At Bombay's Hapkin Institute, founded in 1899, laboratory testing for pneumonic and bubonic plague takes place on a daily basis. Even so, potentially serious outbreaks do occur, most recently in 1995.

Less densely populated rural areas seem unaffected by the disease. For the Irula tribe from the province of Tamil Nadu in southeastern India, rats comprise an important food staple. We may view a diet of rats with disgust, but in several Far Eastern countries rats are considered to be a culinary delicacy. It's a question of cultural bias.

Contrary to popular belief, neither pneumonic nor bubonic plague has been completely eradicated, even in the United States. Though not widely reported, it has occurred in

California, Oregon, Idaho, Nevada, Arizona, New Mexico, Wyoming, Utah, and Colorado. About ten cases are reported annually in the United States, usually in remote areas of the southwest.

Terrier owners who choose to take their dogs into wildlife areas are well advised to heed any warnings they may find posted in the general vicinity of public or private campgrounds and take whatever protective measures are needed for their pets' well-being.

DEN BUILDING AND CARE

It is unlikely that the average person would wish to construct an elaborate, full-size underground den in his or her back yard. For one reason, it takes up a fair amount of space. For another, it's not necessary.

My own den, located at the end of the lawn, replaced a deteriorating, rarely used wooden deck. The dimensions of the U- shaped tunnel, 10 feet × 8 feet × 10 feet, are surprisingly compact and unobtrusive. The size was governed by the space available at the most convenient location and the by presence of a large tree stump.

The 8-foot section and one of the two 10-foot lengths are in the ground. Excluding a 2-foot transition area, the third leg is on the surface.

It would have been simple enough to bury the entire liner, but that would have reduced its versatility. Having only part of it buried allows for easy adaptation from a near full-size den to two smaller training tunnels. A cordless, electric screwdriver and a couple of minutes' work convert it into a straight ten-foot chute, or an oversize Intro-type den complete with one right-angle turn.

The actual liner, constructed from scrap plywood and several two-by-fours used on a previous job, cost virtually nothing but time and effort. Five or six years later it is decidedly

The author's den is only partially buried. The ten-foot section of liner on the left is easily removed to shorten the tunnel for various training purposes. The top of the underground liner was painted to produce a clearer photo. At the upper left-hand corner is a transition area that goes from below to above ground. *Kohler*

An alternative view of the den showing the graded entrance on the near left and the exit on the upper left, at the opposite end of which the slightly elevated transition area is clearly visible. The surface liner is covered with indoor/outdoor carpeting. *Kohler*

weather-worn, but just as functional as the day it was assembled. A reasonable earthdog training tunnel is not a big-ticket item by any means. All you need is yard space.

This is the "short chute" or half tunnel, with one 90 degree turn, without the surface liner. This short-ened version is ideal for training puppies and green youngsters. The area to the left is covered with indoor/outdoor carpeting. The black plastic sheet needed to prevent flooding during the monsoon sea-son in the southwest would work equally well for earthdog enthusiasts in the snow belt. The rocks are used to hold down the plastic. *Kohler*

A standard den liner made from three-quarter-inch exterior plywood. If one plans to haul the den liner from one place to another, it would be more easily handled with a convenient handle attached to the center. *Kohler*

In my case, the surface tunnel and the surrounding area were covered with pseudo grass—indoor/outdoor carpet. In addition to making the whole setup practically invisible from

The liner can easily double as a play tunnel, or be used to coax a reluctant youngster to chase faux quarry. Obviously, it is much easier to do with the help of a partner to hold the puppy and arouse his interest. *Kohler*

20 to 30 feet away, it helps keep weeds in check and dust and mud out of the house.

For the more landscape-conscious, the center space—roughly 12 feet × 10 feet in my situation—can be camouflaged with large pots of flowers or leafy plants or outdoor furniture. In a pinch it could even be used as a base for a small garden shed or greenhouse.

I hesitate to suggest planting a flower bed unless it's well fenced in. If not, dogs will probably destroy it in no time at all. I prefer to have the whole training area fully exposed in order to observe exactly how well the dogs perform.

In order to get dogs accustomed to making both left and right turns, a hinged lid that can be raised or lowered as needed is attached to one of the openings. (It was removed for the photo shoot.)

Cranking a small bicycle wheel to reel in the lure is easier than running with it in tow. For those who are interested in terrier races and plan to participate in coursing, this apparatus also works well for training them to chase the lure. *Kohler*

A number of small holes drilled in the top of the liner allows easy application of a drop or two of air scent which, inside the den, works as well as ground scent. The holes are easily covered with a brick or a rock, should one feel so inclined. For obvious reasons, a certain amount of fresh air must be able to enter training tunnels; liners should not be completely airtight. *Kohler*

Almost any type of barrier can be used at the end of a tunnel. Wire mesh or vertical or horizontal bars work equally well. The author prefers vertical bars about two inches apart, through which a dog can reach and paw at the quarry.

A well-weathered quarry box, complete with lid, positioned at the end of the surface liner—no need to be fancy!

Because I'm not trying to turn my dogs into automatons, I want them to enter via the opening indicated, not necessarily the nearest one. Dogs should not be allowed to develop fixed habits, like using the same opening or repeatedly doing everything exactly the same way each time. It gets too monotonous.

In the final instance, the size and shape of individual training tunnels usually boils down to personal choice and/or feasibility.

Where space is limited, the surface tunnel could easily be placed up against a fence or wall. However, that tends to make the training area small and somewhat restrictive and is best reserved for when there's no alternative.

A basic tunnel liner is constructed of three lengths of half- or three-quarter-inch plywood or one-inch pine boards fastened together to form a three-sided rectangle of manageable length with an interior measurement of approximately nine × nine inches square, or thereabouts (see diagram at end of chapter). The head-liner should rest on top of the sides for added strength and convenient maintenance.

Not only can tunnels vary in size and shape, they need not be buried in order to work. In some parts of the country, keeping liners above ground may be preferable to having them buried. That way they are easy to move from one place to another for exhibitions or training purposes.

Unlike surface liners, the buried liners require periodic maintenance. Depending on where one lives, they may provide convenient if unintentional refuge to all kinds of opportunistic critters.

In addition to valley fever, rattlesnakes, skunks, scorpions and gila monsters, people in Arizona might encounter ticks, tarantulas, black widow or brown recluse spiders, an amazing assortment of stinging ants and the occasional antisocial variety of bees, wasps and hornets.

Dogs are not normally allowed to see or reach the quarry except through the tunnel. However, because it was impossible to photograph this dog's enthusiastic reaction from inside the tunnel we made an exception—not a good thing to do with dogs in training.

"In we go!"

"Gotcha!"

"Next?"

For those with enough space, a second tunnel overgrown with grass and shrubs that resembles a natural wilderness area can be used to further test a dog's determination to go to earth, as well as its scenting ability.

Fortunately for me, my only unpleasant experience with these pesky interlopers was a sudden invasion by red ants. These are mean-tempered rascals that can literally drive dogs crazy!

For town dwellers, it's not as bothersome; out in the desert it's a whole 'nother story. The dangers from wild fauna

There is absolutely no harm and possibly some benefit to allowing a dog to explore the trench before the liner is set in place.

are there for real! The same is true in other states and ten times more so in a natural earth.

Having tunnels with easily removable lids or top sections—screwed down instead of nailed down—makes them easier to inspect the inside on a regular basis. Tunnels should be dismantled and inspected every spring and fall and after

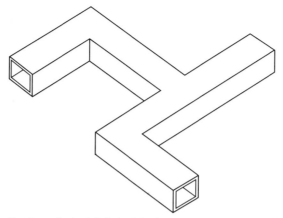

The shape of a den is limited only by the imagination of its designer.

heavy rains—unless completely covered with a tarp—but especially if any dog appears reluctant to enter for no apparent reason.

Dens are a valuable training tool. Keep yours safe and well maintained. Don't let it become a trap for your dogs.

EARTHDOG CARE AND GROOMING

It's surprising how many people who say they care for their dogs really fail to do so. Affection for one's companion animal is an admirable quality, but no guarantee that its basic needs are being adequately addressed. The not-so-subtle difference between "care" and "caring" is easily overlooked.

Grooming is only one type of care. It covers a wide range of disciplines from clipping or stripping a dog's coat to cutting nails and cleaning ears.

For non-showdogs the main reason for grooming is to keep the coat in respectable shape and make the dog look and feel comfortable. The grooming needs of showdogs can be considerably more complicated. Preparing terriers for the show ring is an art form, and as such, is barely relevant to this chapter.

As far as Dachshund coats are concerned, apart from tidying up the straggly hair around the ears, neck and furnishings of the Longhaired variety, brushing and combing when needed, and the occasional minor stripping needed by Wires, most will manage just fine with an occasional bath and the routine hygiene agenda.

Terrier owners are not that lucky. The two methods of grooming harsh-coated terrier breeds are clipping and stripping. Clipping away the coat, and sometimes the furnishings, is done with electric clippers. Stripping entails the manual

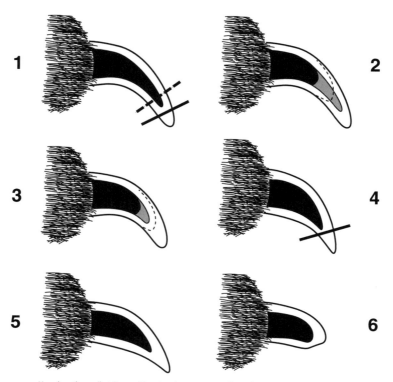

Keeping the nails trim, neither too long nor too short, is an essential part of an earthdog's care. Long, neglected nails can make walking, running and digging painful. Only when the nails are kept short can they be cut or clipped without bleeding. Illustration #1 shows a long nail with an equally long "quick," or vein that carries the blood supply. The longer the nail, the longer the quick. If cut at the bottom line shown in the diagram, the quick will not bleed but the nail will remain too long. If cut at the top line, the nail will bleed superficially. The nail will still be long, but the quick will begin to recede. Illustrations #2 and #3 show how the quick recedes as the nail is shortened with regular trimming once or twice each week. Illustration #4 indicates the appropriate point and angle at which to cut the nail to retain the desired length, after the quick has receded. Illustration #5 indicates acceptable length of nails for earthdogs, while Illustration #6 shows the length preferred for the nails of the "well-shod" show dog.

removal of part of the coat, known as the jacket, using a special tool called a stripping knife. When the hair is pulled out by hand, the method is then known as plucking.

If you don't trim your own dog, clipping is available at any grooming shop. Stripping, aside from being more arduous, involves greater skill, and is a correspondingly costlier service. It is a totally different procedure and not always

When a wirehaired dog starts looking this ragged, it's time to top the coat or strip it out altogether.

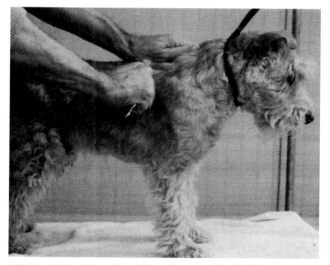

A light sprinkling of grooming chalk on the coat makes the job easier. Start at the withers and, bracing the dog's skin firmly with one hand, strip out the surplus dead or blown coat with the other hand or with a stripping knife as you prefer. Study a good grooming book or video and watch an expert at work if you can before you try it yourself. Stripping takes time and practice, so be patient, learn from your mistakes and you should eventually grasp the time-honored skill.

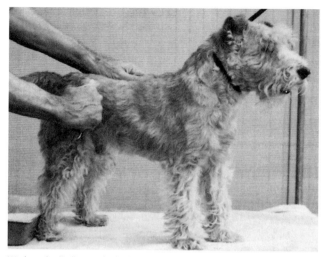

Work methodically over the body, neck and head. After that, comb out the beard and leg furnishings.

Brush, comb and pick at the dog's body coat and furnishings daily for about eight to twelve weeks and the results may surprise you.

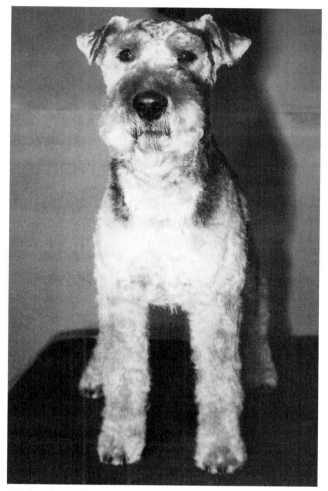

This champion Welsh Terrier is groomed for den work.

readily available except from professional handlers or terrier people who participate in conformation events.

Hand-stripped terriers are rarely seen outside the show ring, unless the owner undertakes the work personally or hires an expert. With a little effort and sufficient practice, stripping out a coat is not a difficult skill to acquire.

The advantage of stripping (even when badly done) is that the new coat grows back harsh and wiry and retains its

color. A clipped coat quickly loses its natural color and text-
ure and in most cases takes on a rather bland appearance.
Basically it's a matter of personal preference, but a clipped
dog just doesn't look the same.

This chapter is less concerned with cosmetic grooming
than with general care and management. It is better for the
dog to be clipped than neglected. True or not, an unkempt
dog tends to reflect negatively on its owner's concern and
attachment for the animal.

Neophyte earthdog enthusiasts may be unaware of the
type of problems dogs might encounter at a dig. Although the
test site itself may have been thoroughly cleared, problems
can still occur and hazards can be present throughout the
entire area.

Depending on where one lives, fleas, ticks and other
external parasites may be common problems. Preventive
applications of flea and tick repellent help to ward off problems before they begin.

To avoid bringing unwanted external parasites home,
dogs should be carefully examined for "hitchhikers," treated
with an appropriate pesticide, if necessary, and brushed and
combed before leaving the test site.

Because den trials frequently take place in rural or semi-
rural locations, watch out for broken glass, thorns, grass
seeds, burrs, stickers and foxtails that easily attach to dogs'
feet or become embedded in their coats.

Look and feel between the dog's pads and toes, under-
neath the "armpits," and between its hind legs. Don't over-
look its ears and beard (if any).

To avoid becoming a victim yourself, it is a good idea to
remove prickly burrs with tweezers and a fine comb.

While an earthdog will probably never need to use its
teeth at a trial, a terrier facing quarry should be equipped to
deal with it. Strong, sound teeth are vital to any earthdog and
their care is a matter of the greatest importance. Dog owners

are slowly becoming aware that canine dental care helps to assure continued good health in dogs as much as in humans. Dogs rarely require the same extensive dental treatment as their owners, but will certainly benefit from periodic dental care, especially as they grow older.

Dogs are subject to a variety of dental problems, including tartar buildup, cavities, gum infections, abscesses, loose teeth and retained baby teeth. The last is probably one of the more common problems.

As a rule, dogs have 28 deciduous or "milk" teeth and 42 permanent ones. Retained milk teeth should be extracted by the time the puppy is four or five months old to avoid possible development of any bite faults. Such extractions are easily done without anesthetics that might endanger a puppy's life. However, be guided by your veterinarian on when and how to do this.

An earthdog's feet are his fortune, figuratively speaking. For his comfort, well-being and ability to work, the feet should be checked regularly. Hair and debris should be removed from between the pads and toes to minimize any foot discomfort.

Too often I have seen dogs with mud and matted hair packed firmly between their toes and under their pads. The discomfort these dogs experience is comparable to a person with a stone in his boot.

An earthdog's nails should be cut reasonably short, but not amputated. It is best to cut the nails several days before an event. In case you should happen to hit a quick or two, there will be time enough for any soreness to dissipate. To avoid that, nails can be filed or ground down on a weekly basis.

Don't forget to check those dew claws; some dogs have them and some don't. There's little doubt in my mind that the nails at the front grow faster than those at the back.

Clean the ears on a regular basis and before and after a trial. I prefer ear cream or powder to watery products. If the

Den work is anything but sanitary. Even shorthaired dogs will benefit from a bath after a typical session underground.

ears have a discharge, smell bad, or appear infected then you should see your vet.

Dogs can also get dirt and dust in their eyes just as we do, maybe more so being nearer to the ground. Make sure the eyes are kept clean and free of foreign objects. Wipe away any discharge from the corners of the eyes and apply eye drops formulated for dogs when needed.

Keeping one's earthdog in tiptop shape is part of the drill. The healthier the dog, the better he'll work, the better he'll feel and the more you'll enjoy your time together.

17

OUTDOOR TERRIERS AND DACHSHUNDS

There are a wide variety of excellent, relatively inexpensive outdoor kennels currently available. I particularly like the plastic models that are easy to maintain, easy to keep clean and practically indestructible. Even so, some people prefer to rely on their own ingenuity and build something from scratch. So be it!

Regardless of the type of construction, a good doghouse should be insulated against both heat and cold and be completely weatherproof. In addition to walls and a roof, it is probably even more important to insulate the floor. This is truly a critical detail all too frequently overlooked.

Although they've been used for years, steel drums, regardless of modifications or alterations, do not make acceptable dog houses. Metal conducts both heat and cold much too readily for that.

For small to medium-sized terriers I suggest a snug, insulated, wooden structure about three feet wide, two feet deep, and barely high enough to allow the occupant to stand upright.

The actual sleeping quarters might be roughly two feet square, with the remaining space forming the entryway. The sleeping area and the entryway should be divided by a removable partition, or baffle, in order to help eliminate harmful drafts and keep the bedding in place. It is best for the roof to be hinged so it can be raised for easy cleaning.

Bedding is largely a matter of choice. Cedar shavings make the best bedding because, changed frequently enough, it tends to discourage external parasites. However, clean straw, regular wood shavings, rags or even shredded newspaper is better than a bare floor. For colder climates an insulated heating pad may be appropriate.

Depending on where one lives, dogs require about 50 percent more bedding in winter than in summer. A lot depends on what they are accustomed to having.

There are pros and cons to keeping dogs chained outdoors, or confined to pens for that matter. Neither is highly recommended, but sometimes it's unavoidable.

Most, but not all, dogs thrive best when living in the home as part of the family. When that becomes impractical, it is essential that the dog be trained and exercised daily. Its existence should not be confined to so many square feet of run, or to the amount of ground it can cover on the end of a length of chain.

For earthdog breeds, permanent runs should be at least four feet wide and ten to twelve feet long, or even more if possible. Run surfaces can be packed dirt, concrete, patio blocks, blacktop, pea gravel or common red brick. Perhaps the most popular run surface is concrete, which is fine providing it is sufficiently sloped for good drainage.

Blacktop has few, if any, advantages. It gets hot and sticky in summer and is absolutely not recommended. I've seen such runs and didn't like them one bit.

In most cases, common red brick laid over a bed of sand works great. It drains well, dries quickly and is easy on the dog's feet.

Quarter-inch screened pea gravel over packed dirt is good, too, but not for dogs that like to dig.

A raised bedboard or pallet should be provided for dogs to sleep on, along with ample shade available during hot, sunny weather—although the early morning sun is always beneficial.

Dogs normally kept outdoors should not be subjected to abrupt temperature changes, as might happen to dogs taken into an air-conditioned building in summer, or heated homes or garages in winter. Sudden, extreme changes could cause a dog's built-in thermostat to malfunction, doing him more harm than good.

During very cold weather, extra fat should be added to the diet. During hot spells, dogs are naturally inclined to eat less. This should not cause undue concern unless accompanied by symptoms of illness.

A plentiful supply of fresh drinking water should remain available, winter and summer alike. Keep water bowls clean and sanitary to prevent harmful bacteria build-up. Some dogs are inclined to spill their drinking water; a weighted water bowl should offset that.

If a dog must be chained out, be sure that the chain is a reasonable size. I've seen small dogs on the type of chain that might be used to tow a ten-ton truck. Tie-out chains require at least two swivels to prevent them from becoming twisted.

Don't chain a dog out on a slip collar; he could choke himself to death. Use strong, pliable leather or nylon collars that are not apt to make a dog's neck sore from constant friction.

Check collars and chains every day. Don't fasten the chain to the collar with twisted bailing wire (people do this as a safeguard, in case the snap should break). Not only can it wear away the hair and skin around the neck, the sharp ends have been know to get imbedded in the flesh, causing deep, painful lacerations.

Used correctly, an overhead running cable keeps dogs from having to drag a chain around all day and offers some additional freedom of movement.

Most dog owners have no intention of mistreating their pets, but mishaps have a way of happening unless one stays alert. Don't be the one caught napping. Check often, making certain your outside dog is not in any kind of trouble due to heat or cold, or lack of food and water.

Dogs (and cats) allowed to run loose without proper restraint or supervision can only complicate the already alarming problems of animal control and pet pollution. Make sure your dog is not one of these.

Unsupervised animals bother neighbors, injure children, get hurt in fights or are killed by cars. Some may be responsible for spreading diseases.

Most cities and towns in the United States have dog ordinances that define the maximum number of dogs permitted each household and stipulate the conditions under which dogs may be kept. These ordinances may vary from one community to another. Dog owners are well advised to learn exactly what their local ordinances do and do not allow and act in compliance.

It is safe to assume that, regardless of where you live, you will be held responsible for any personal injury or destruction of property caused by your dog. It is imperative to keep one's dog under complete control at all times. In my book, that absolutely includes reducing nuisance barking to a minimum, which makes an important contribution to peaceful coexistence with one's neighbors.

Those who choose to keep a dog have an obligation to care for it in a humane fashion. Keeping your outside dog under constant supervision helps to ensure he remains fit and healthy and ready to participate at Earthdog Tests.

18

MEDICAL PROBLEMS AND FIELD INJURIES FOR EARTHDOGS AND THEIR HANDLERS

In the course of preparing for and participating in Earthdog Tests, mishaps and injuries are bound to happen, regardless of how careful we are. This chapter will describe some of the common slipups with which earthdog fans must cope and what they can do about them.

ANIMAL BITES OR WOUNDS (HUMAN)

The latest medical recommendations suggest that anyone bitten by a dog or other animal adopt the following procedure: If the injury is serious the victim should receive prompt, expert medical treatment by trained trauma professionals. Treatment for serious bite injuries should conform to the Zook-Miller protocol for such injuries, including: flushing out wounds with large quantities of pressured saline, meticulous wound and wound edge debridement (removal of all injured or contaminated tissue), primary wound closure (stitches), adequate antibiotic treatment, close postoperative care and plastic surgery, if needed.

Initially there is a difference between a serious and a life-threatening injury. However, based on one's resources and whereabouts, e.g., remote wilderness areas where one should never go alone but many do, any significant injury may become potentially life-threatening. Keep in mind that to a debilitated person "a remote wilderness area" may be no more than a few hundred yards from a major highway. The solution is to never venture into any wilderness area without at least one other human companion.

COLITIS

Inflammatory bowel disease is the most common form of chronic colitis; it makes traveling with your dog a chore. Possible causes are many, ranging from allergic reactions to genetic predisposition. Irritable bowel syndrome, a non-inflammatory disorder, is frequently associated with high stress levels. Relief from a stressful environment, tranquilizers, increased dietary fiber and drugs to block impulses to the parasympathetic nerves are commonly used remedies.

CONJUNCTIVITIS

Conjunctivitis is a fancy term for "runny eyes." The causes range from summer allergies, simple irritation, dust, toxic fumes, viral or bacterial infection and more. Dogs should not be permitted to ride with their heads out of car windows in order to prevent foreign objects from blowing into their eyes—a prime, avoidable cause of the problem. Other known causes of recurring eye irritation should be avoided as much as possible. Dogs working in natural earths should have their eyes checked after each excursion.

CUT PADS

It is possible for dogs to cut their pads on broken glass or other sharp objects almost anytime. Suturing is not a great idea because the stitches can be ripped out and make the laceration that much worse. A bandage protected by a leather boot and antibiotics to prevent infection seem to work about as well as anything else. Discuss your options with your vet.

HEATSTROKE OR HEAT PROSTRATION

Heatstroke or heat prostration may occur at any time and any place during hot, humid weather. The latter is the less dangerous of the two. Overexertion during an Earthdog Test, too much sun or confinement inside inadequately ventilated vehicles are open invitations to trouble. The onset is characterized by rapid breathing, excessive salivation and/or sudden collapse. Victims may gag or vomit, and develop a staring or startled expression.

Breaking car windows to free distressed animals is now legal in many states. Since there is rarely enough time to locate the owner, such a break-in could possibly save a dog's life. Unfortunately, uninformed bystanders have been known to watch stricken dogs die, assuming they'd gone mad.

Victims should be placed in the shade, made to rest quietly and splashed with cool water or covered with a wet towel. An ice pack or a damp cloth on his head and neck helps lower body temperature. Small quantities of water or ice cubes to lick are permissible, but large drinks of cold water should not be given. The dog should be allowed to rest in a cool but not necessarily air-conditioned place until signs of distress have somewhat subsided and then transported to the nearest emergency veterinary clinic.

INJURY AND SHOCK

Almost any accident resulting in physical injury and pain can induce shock. Blood pressure drops and the pulse becomes weak and rapid. Gums grow pale, almost gray in color. Shallow breathing is punctuated by sharp gasps. A dog may appear subdued or be in a state of collapse and have sunken, staring eyes.

An injured dog must be kept quiet and quickly taken to the nearest veterinary clinic or emergency care center. With the most severe injury, prompt treatment is required to pre-vent shock. Broken limbs, if any, must be gently supported while the dog is being moved. Attempting to reduce or repo-sition broken limbs should not be attempted by the lay person.

External bleeding should always be stopped or mini-mized. Bleeding from external orifices indicates internal injuries. The prescription is "PIE": pressure, ice and eleva-tion. Apply evenly sustained hand **P**ressure to the wound with gauze, a towel or whatever else is handy. Apply **I**ce when it's available. **E**levate the injured area as far above the level of the head as conditions allow.

Handle all injured dogs with caution, including your own. A dog that has been injured or is in shock may be disoriented and confused. In such condition, it could fail to recognize its owner and try to attack. Given the right cir-cumstances, all dogs are potential biters. A significant number of dog injuries could be avoided if owners realized that young animals learn to deal with their environment through experience. Due to their natural curiosity, puppies are at greatest risk of injury anyplace that is not "puppy proofed."

About 75 percent of these injuries fall into one of three cat-egories: 1) motor vehicle accidents; 2) animal interaction (fighting); 3) unknown causes. Bitches have more falls from high places, or are crushed or burned. Males "interact" much too frequently for their own good.

LAMENESS

Excluding injuries, the most frequent causes of lameness in dogs are arthritis, hip dysplasia, overexercise, strains, sprains and foreign objects stuck to the bottom of the feet. Except for the latter, rest and recovery are a package deal.

OBESITY

As high as 44 percent of all dogs are estimated to be overweight, compared to the 3.5 percent estimated to be underweight. Den dogs should be "lean and mean," not fat. Obese dogs can benefit from low-energy, low-fat diets that aid in weight stabilization. An overweight den dog would not be worth much at work or in a trial and should be put on a diet to improve his performance, general health and life expectancy.

RINGWORM

Less common than it once was, ringworm is characterized by the classic round or semicircular hairless lesions that appear on any body part. Highly contagious to humans, it responds well to antifungal and antibiotic therapy. Ringworm is a fungal disease, not a worm. Infection is confirmed with a Wood's lamp (a diagnostic device uses that ultraviolet light) or from laboratory cultures. Ringworm is fairly common in domestic farm animals. However, the possibility of a dog contracting an infection while participating in an Earthdog Test on farm property is remote.

SEBORRHEA

Primary idiopathic seborrhea occurs in several terrier breeds. The condition is characterized by the excess production of sebum (a skin oil). The symptoms include greasy deposits of yellowish-brown scales on the skin and coat and a rancid, disagreeable odor. Primary idiopathic seborrhea may be due to a genetic predisposition in affected breeds. In most instances, with appropriate therapy the condition is controllable but not curable.

SEIZURES

Seizures, also called fits, are reasonably common in puppies and older dogs of certain breeds. Seizures may stem from numerous causes, including brain tumors and heredity predisposition to epilepsy. Most seizures are effectively controlled with medication. Terriers are no more predisposed to seizures than most other breeds.

"Scottie cramp" (less common than it once was) is a severe seizure that mimics epilepsy usually induced by abnormally vigorous or prolonged exercise in predisposed individuals. These abnormal muscle spasms are breed-specific, and possibly due to extreme lactic acid overload. Allowing a dog to rest quietly until its metabolism has stabilized is usually sufficient. If in doubt, consult your vet.

SKUNK OR PUTRID ODOR

The product most frequently used by professional dog groomers to neutralize offensive odors is Massengill™ feminine douche, available at all drugstores. Soak the coat for 15 minutes or more before rinsing. Repeat as needed. Skunk Kleen™ is one of several new skunk odor neutralizers on the market. Follow label directions. The often highly touted tomato juice remedy rarely works, but baking soda does, sometimes, as will several washings with Dial™ soap.

As skunks are a prime reservoir for rabies in the wild, it seems wisest to keep dogs well away from the smelly critters. Every active earthdog should always be protected from rabies. If you are also planning to take your dog hunting, wilderness hiking or camping, make sure he receives a rabies booster first.

SNAKE BITES

In the event that your dog is bitten by a poisonous snake, the first order of business is to remain calm and keep the dog still and quiet. Depending on the type of snake and location of the wound, dogs are reasonably resistant to most snake venom, but that's a generalization. General symptoms include swelling, edema, tissue sloughing, necrosis (dead tissue), pain on or near the wound, drooling and perhaps lameness.

Treatment includes administering polyvalent antivenin, supported by shock, pain and infection control as needed. Neutralizing the venom within four hours of the attack is considered critical. Freezing the site to slow venom-circulation

214

time has proven to be ineffective. Do not open up or cut into a bite wound. Do not attempt to suck out the venom; you may poison yourself. Finally, get your dog to a veterinarian— pronto!

VALLEY FEVER

Cryptococcus is an opportunistic fungus found in parts of California and most of the desert Southwest. Dormant fungus spores that have been moisture activated are released into the air by the winds that follow the rainy season. Spores are inhaled into the lungs by normal breathing. Most mammals living in these desert regions for any length of time are eventually infected. Dogs and humans are at equal risk.

Valley fever, known by several other names, causes flu-like symptoms: persistent fever, labored breathing, dry cough, loss of appetite, depression, enlarged lymph nodes, heavy nasal discharge and lameness. Strong, healthy dogs may recover without the owners realizing they were sick. Those with compromised immune systems are rarely so lucky. A sick dog exposed to valley fever while at an Earthdog Test might easily be misdiagnosed by a veterinarian unfamiliar with the symptoms of the disease—not easily diagnosed even by experts. Because the dormant spore exists primarily 12 inches below the ground's surface, valley fever is of significant concern to all earthdog enthusiasts living in the arid desert regions of the southwestern United States.

The puppy you buy for Earthdog Tests will be your source of pleasure for many years to come. You will always get more pleasure from participating in Earthdog Tests by keeping the instinctive nature of your dog's performance in the proper perspective. That's the fairest approach to you and your puppy as you proceed in this exciting performance activity.

19

ENJOYING THE SPORT

Anyone who plans to attend a dig solely for the purpose of obtaining a qualifying score on his or her earthdog will miss half the fun. Because much of the action occurs underground, Earthdog Tests, per se, are not an ideal spectator sport. It is far better to view the tests as a social event that, as a bonus, provides the more fortunate participants with a measure of self-satisfaction. One should enjoy the simple pleasure of participating and the opportunity to make new friends. Being a part of the earthdog fraternity is a win-win situation if ever there was one, regardless of the eventual outcome of the test(s).

At a recent Earthdog Test, a doctor friend of mine was smiling and possibly more cheerful after his dog failed to qualify than some of those whose dogs performed much better. A more intense fellow participant, puzzled by this unusual display of misplaced joviality, casually remarked, "You appear to be having a hell of a good time, under the circumstances!" "Why not?" my friend replied. "The dog didn't perform that well, but nobody died!"

I can like a person who knows his or her priorities and keeps things in the proper perspective. As Americans, we seem to have developed an obsession with winning and a need for instant gratification that, for some, completely circumvents the joy of participating. It really shouldn't be that way.

As a former runner, watching the running of the 100th Boston Marathon on sports TV, I marveled as exhausted, physically challenged athletes stumbled triumphantly across the finish line many hours behind the winners. For those and others like them, participation was in itself a magnificent accomplishment. It represented a moment of personal triumph destined to last a lifetime, even in today's jaded society. In fact, during a retrospective of the previous 99 Boston Marathons, noted TV personality Ted Koppel admitted that the experience of "running and finishing a marathon" had afforded him one of the moments of greatest pleasure in his life.

Earthdog Tests may not be in the same league as a marathon, but the positive or negative mind-set is surprisingly similar. Goal-setting is an excellent way to gage one's personal success. How far do you plan to go in the sport and how much effort will you expend to make it happen? Establishing the ultimate goal and breaking it down into smaller, more readily attainable increments is the easiest way to go. Here's one example:

1) Short-term goal
2) Mid-term goal
3) Final goal
4) Maintenance goal

The Short-Term Goal: The short-term goal for an absolute beginner in the sport might be to compile a list of essential requirements, choose a breed, and buy a puppy. That would be a good start.

Compile a schedule, write it down, and set deadlines. Keep an accurate record of your accomplishments. Document but ignore setbacks; focus on moving up to the next level. Keep trying and something good is bound to happen. It sounds trite, but it works. Plan and implement each phase and move on. Evaluate and modify: Add something here, subtract something there, remembering to enjoy yourself in the process. Enjoyment shouldn't have to wait until next time; there may not be a next time. Stay focused but flexible enough to take advantage of unforeseen opportunities to move ahead of schedule.

One of many probable scenarios might be: Learn all you can about the breed you have chosen. Establish an obtainable, realistic training and conditioning program. Seek help when needed. Contact a local earthdog or all-breed club in your area. Attending a few meetings as a guest and getting to know the members before you decide to join a club is always a smart idea, too.

Mid-term Goal: Learn to train and handle your dog correctly. Attend den trials or exhibitions. Find a training companion with whom you can work. Start collecting trial essentials.

Final Goal: Enter your dog at every Earthdog Test you can find. Keep your expectations low and your hopes high. It's better to be pleasantly surprised than sadly disillusioned.

Make your final goal an attainable one. Achieving Junior Earthdog, Senior Earthdog or Master Earthdog status should be of less importance than the satisfaction of attaining your initial goal. Whatever else you accomplish beyond that is a bonus.

Maintenance Goal: Continue participating and having fun until you lose interest or decide to move on to bigger and better things, whichever the case may be.

Go prepared to enjoy the entire spectacle, not only your own participation. Comparative beginners should watch the experts and learn what they can from them. Yeah, perceptual learning works for all of us. Novices should be mindful that not everything that veterans do works equally as well for beginners.

Failure to qualify the first or second time around is no great tragedy, unless you choose to make it one. Don't get down on yourself or your dog and don't take your disappointments home. Leave them at the trial grounds where they belong.

Always arrive at an event well in advance of the scheduled time. Having to rush around at the last minute can be unsettling for both dog and handler. A good rule of thumb is to arrive early and stay late.

As Earthdog Tests cater mainly to dogs, their accompanying owners may have to make do as best they can unless they go self-contained and fully prepared. That is doubly true if the weather fails to cooperate. Take no chances. Think of it as a camping trip and go prepared for any eventuality. Pack your own food, drink, and shelter. Wear comfortable shoes and seasonably appropriate clothing. Rain, wind, and cold can be annoying and so can the heat. Summer showers or sudden thunderstorms can turn a grassy field into a messy quagmire. Inexpensive tarps, plastic rain wear, and lightweight overshoes can prove to be useful items to have along.

You may be on your feet all day; pack an extra pair of comfortable shoes. High heels for women are totally out of place, even for spectators. The soft ground at outdoor venues can make walking in heels extremely difficult. Carry your own folding chairs so you can sit as close to the action as possible in comparative comfort.

When traveling by car in winter, take enough blankets to keep everyone warm should your vehicle break down in a remote area, especially at night, or if snow drifts, flash floods or mud slides close the highways.

During the hot summer months take along shade cloth, a cooler and plenty of ice and drinking water. If you intend to leave your dog in your vehicle for any length of time, don't—unless you have an air-conditioned motor home. Even then, make spot checks to ensure the generator is fully operational. Many dogs die annually from the heat under supposedly ideal conditions.

In most cases, dogs are better off outside the vehicle in the shade of a tree or under a tarp or awning. Dogs going from air-conditioned comfort into the blazing hot sun can become ultra-sensitive to the heat due to the abrupt contrast in temperatures. Those minus the luxury of a self-contained motor home should remove the crate or crates from their vehicles and stand them in a well-ventilated, shaded area to give the dog(s) time to acclimate. A lightweight tent or awning can be mighty handy. If necessary, spritz your dog's coat with water from a spray bottle or drape him in a damp towel. Give dogs a large lump of ice to lick in place of large quantities of drinking water.

Although drinking water is generally available at the test site, it is a good idea to bring your own. It's surprising how fussy dogs can be away from home. Some may refuse to drink unfamiliar water because the difference in the mineral content affects the taste. Others may drink it and get an upset stomach. Either way, we'd all rather be safe than sorry.

If you really want to enjoy the new sport, learn to become a total participant. Go with the intention of having a good time no matter what and chances are, you will.

A "house cur" following in the steps of a farm boy. House curs may well have been the first earthdog breeds. Centuries past, dogs were classified according to their abilities, not by their appearances.

A SECOND LOOK AT TERRIER EVOLUTION

The precise origin of the earliest earthdogs remains uncertain. What we do know is that most terrier breeds originated within the British Isles during a broad time frame that encompassed the Roman, Viking, and Norman conquests. The question is: How, when, where and why?

Hunting, as such, neither originated in nor was limited to the British Isles. Pursuing game of one kind or another with hounds, whether on horseback or on foot, dates back to antiquity and is regarded as a universal pursuit involving many kinds of dogs—earthdogs included.

Centuries prior to his developing the pursuit of foxes for sport, man sought wild game for food. In addition, because foxes did not and do not exist naturally in all parts of the world, global development of fox hunting was not possible. Even in England, the fox didn't became popular quarry until the 17th century. By then horses and hounds were able to race across the open grassland that was once impenetrable forests. It wasn't until after the great forests had fallen to the woodsman's axe, so noblemen could erect their huge wooden castles along the border of Scotland to the north and Wales to the west, that pleasure hunting became a popular diversion of the ruling class. Many earlier events in Britain impacted the nature of sport hunting long before the sporting gentlemen of the 19th century donned their top hats and pink coats and the now-venerable hunts like the Quorn, Pytchley, Cottesmore, Belvior and Fernie came into being.

SOCIETAL INFLUENCES IN ENGLISH HISTORY

In a way, the evolution of terriers stands as an enduring tribute to the guile and determination of these native island people and their ability to survive despite the extreme cruelty and brutality of centuries of feudal rule known as the Dark Ages. Enforced servitude, oppression, extreme poverty and starvation common to the times undoubtedly played a large part in how terriers were first developed and utilized in Great Britain.

Under the feudal rule of Kings Canute and William the Conqueror during the 10th and 11th centuries, respectively, barons, lords, landholders, vassals, villagers, farmers, peasants, serfs and indentured slaves lived only to serve their master, the king. Naturally, some lived considerably better than others. For non-history buffs, the feudal system was the world's first "pyramid scheme." The ruling classes at the top of the heap raked in the goodies; the laboring classes at the bottom did all the work and got nothing. Not a very equitable arrangement, neither then nor now!

In addition to other gross injustices, around A.D. 975 Canute enacted The Forest Game Laws, making hunting and coursing deer and hare the exclusive privilege of the nobility and the upper social classes. Later, William the Conqueror would go one better than Canute by confiscating huge tracts of land as his personal hunting preserve. Peasants, husbandmen and their families living within those boundaries were ruthlessly evicted and their homes destroyed. Known as the New Forest, it was designated as land where only the king and his retinue could hunt. The penalty for poaching or merely trespassing on the king's playground was death or disfigurement.

For countless generations thereafter British serfs, peasants, free-born men and the laboring classes were not only prohibited from hunting, but deprived of owning a hound. To obtain a lease from a "landlord," feudal husbandmen and tenant farmers (equivalent to American sharecroppers) were pledged not to own or house a hound or lurcher, or discharge a firearm except to frighten rooks and crows away from newly planted fields. ("Lurcher," an archaic Old English word for thief, was the name given to terrier/sight hound crossbreeds frequently used by poachers to catch game illegally.) Tenants who reneged on their word were promptly evicted and their hounds "expeditated"—intentionally maimed by removing their foot pads and sometimes their toes to prevent deer chasing. With arable land in short supply, eviction was tantamount to a sentence of death by starvation for the culprits and their families.

Commoners and serfs were permitted to own drover or herding curs or small house curs. This was because these small, generic dogs were needed to work livestock and their hunting potential was greatly underestimated. Moreover, based on the erroneous belief that dogs needed their tails to act as rudders—enabling them to turn sharply at top speed while in pursuit of game—all barnyard dogs were docked.

THE BEGINNINGS OF TERRIER EVOLUTION

It seems quite feasible that the first terriers were probably "house curs," as small, nondescript dogs were then known. In *Dogs* (1839), author C. H. Smith expressed a similar belief when he wrote:

> Nor is the arrangement of placing the terrier race at the head of our cur dogs to be rejected . . . *Cur* is only a mutation of the Celtic *Cu*, the Greek *Kuon*, and even the Latin *Canis*, all emphatically pointing to the most ancient and general [common] name of the dog in Europe.

One might correctly suppose that at one point the earliest terriers' most important role was to control all manner of vermin in and around the homestead. Not only did these lowly regarded canines effectively control vermin, they became extremely efficient hunters or, more accurately, many a starving family's meal ticket. So desperate was the lot of these people that if their dogs failed to provide a meal, they could well become a meal themselves.

POACHING

Much like their masters, dogs were expected to earn their keep every day and in every way. Not only did they live to hunt, they hunted to live. For the next several centuries, poaching was a necessary, if hazardous, way for greatly impoverished country folk to feed their families.

It wasn't necessary to be caught in the act in order to be punished. Based on the notion that the thought preceded the deed, anyone found to be in possession of a net or snare could be arrested and summarily judged guilty of intent to commit a crime. On the other hand, a fleeing dog needed to be caught and identified before the owner could be punished.

Over the centuries, poachers and their dogs were familiar figures in traditional rural life throughout much of the British Isles. As one might expect, ancient historical accounts rarely corroborate the tales recounted in the social contacts of normal village life and vice versa. To assume that either version is 100 percent accurate and unbiased would be naive. Notwithstanding, there's little doubt that in a land with no written language of its own during its early history, oral tradition preceded the written word by a considerable margin.

It was folklorists, story tellers and wandering troubadours who first recounted memorable events, often in song and rhyme. Some of these accounts remain as part of our culture in various forms. In many instances it may have been two or three centuries after actual occurrences before learned scribes picked up their quills and wrote their politically or religiously motivated interpretations of past events into the history books of their time.

Terrier history also was divided into two almost irreconcilable versions: written history and the oral tradition that affected all of the rural life. We can take it from there. In the semi-rural English community where I grew up, the poacher and his dog were part of the culture. For that reason alone I tend to believe that, until quite recently, the historical value of ancient folklore was too readily dismissed by the majority of sophisticated historians.

Most conflicting accounts of past events that occurred in ancient Britain seemed to stem from the vast social gap that segregated the British upper and lower classes for countless generations. It is a gap not well-bridged even today. Even as England slowly emerged from the often brutal oppression of feudalism and embarked on a more enlightened era, the ancient game laws favorable to land owners were not repealed and suppression simply replaced oppression.

Wealthy owners of large country estates retained gamekeepers to raise and preserve the game on their land and curtail poaching. Prior to 1827, man-traps and spring guns were used to apprehend and maim intruders and otherwise deter poaching or trespassing on private property. Poachers retaliated by attacking the gamekeepers. Fatalities occurred on both sides.

Gamekeeper's bandogs, so named because they were chained up by day and released at night, were an additional hazard for the poachers to deal with. These included savage Mastiffs, descendants of dogs the Normans called Alaunts, the original dogs of war first mentioned in the Forest Laws of King Canute. Their quarry was poachers. Poachers countered by training their dogs to hunt alone, mostly at night, and return home with the day's catch—or at least part of it! Another way of minimizing the risk of personal injury or apprehension for the poacher was still-hunting. To reduce the waiting process, semi-domesticated ferrets were used to bolt rabbits from their warrens for the dogs to catch.

CLUES IN LITERATURE

The valuable role played by dogs in the lives of both the higher and lower British social strata before and during the 18th and 19th centuries is not always found in books written in French or Latin for the better educated. More reliable sources are books and documents that otherwise depict the tenor of everyday life within the British Isles. These books provide rare snippets of information about the daily activities of the "laboring class" and their dogs, not to be found elsewhere.

The History of Everyday Things In England (1933), by Marjorie and C. H. B. Quennell, contains an illustration from the early 1800s depicting a small terrier-type "turnspit" dog at work. The dog is shown running on a small treadmill, operating a turnspit in a tavern kitchen at Newcastle Emlyn in South Wales. The treadmill itself is attached to a relatively

The lot of the turnspit dog (shown at the top of this print) in early England was anything but happy.

low ceiling, slightly to one side of a large open fireplace—where the heat was undoubtedly most intense.

There is no indication how long a turnspit dog was made to work the treadmill. Presumably until the meat was cooked; perhaps several hours, perhaps all day, depending on the size of the roast.

THE MENACE OF RATS

In spite of the fox's fearsome reputation, both real and fanciful, rats have always been far more abundant, widespread and destructive than all other species of vermin combined. Poachers and predators may have been the gamekeepers' nemesis, but vermin in general and rats in particular were everyone's problem.

Before modern methods of pest control were developed, keeping vermin in check was more a necessity than a sport. Terriers were one of the major means of dealing with rats in centuries past. Frequently kept in the home at night, they would be turned out during the day in search of rats. Those early terriers became a common sight in barns, stables, warehouses, and wherever rats might be found, and were greatly valued for their ability to make short work of even the largest wharf rats, some frequently too big for cats to handle.

Much has been written about what we call "dog sports." It's unfortunate that using dogs to hunt and kill vermin has been so widely depicted as sport, when for many generations it was a vital necessity. According to an ancient Welsh homily, "The house is a good secret (safe) place, for fear of the terrier." Hopefully, Earthdog Tests will prove that, given the chance, modern earthdog breeds are worthy descendants of their highly utilitarian forebears.

THE MOUNTED HUNT IN A CHANGING WORLD

The fox has always been among the most universally vilified predators. Known to kill newborn lambs, raid hen houses and destroy game birds' nests, European farmers still regard the fox with much the same animosity that cattle- and sheepmen in the western United States display towards wolves and coyotes.

During England's colonial era "when the sun never set on the British Empire," some members of British society's upper strata came to revere fox hunting as a near–religious experience. A youth was not considered a true huntsman until he was "blooded," or smeared with fox blood, and awarded a "brush" (tail) or "mask" (head) at the satisfactory conclusion of a successful hunt.

High ranking British military officers, both active and retired, were an integral part of the venerable fox hunting fraternity. The very individuals responsible for Britain's dominion over a fourth of the world's population during that time, *Pukka sahibs,* reveled in past glories amidst the fruits of plenty. Governed by strict tradition, the mounted hunt was an important and prestigious institution in the social fabric of the time. An ultra-exclusive club, membership was limited to the cream of the English gentry, both military and civilian.

Fox hunting was introduced into the United States by Lord Fairfax, who settled in Virginia in 1742 and imported hounds from England. In 1766 the Gloucester Foxhound Club near Philadelphia, Pennsylvania, was formed, then one at Hempstead, Long Island in 1770, followed by the Brooklyn Hunt in 1789. Hunts eventually spread throughout the midwest and Canada. Although some huntsmen brought hunting servants from England and rode to the hounds according to venerable English tradition, in the United States "hunting" became and has remained an equestrian event.

THE RESOURCEFUL FOX

Unfortunately for the participants, during the hunt the wily fox, using its legendary survival skills, had the annoying habit of retreating into inaccessible dens and "laying up" at the most inconvenient time.

To forestall a premature end to a good day's sport, and the occasional brilliant display of horsemanship and bravado, a "hole stopper," familiar with the local terrain, went ahead prior to the hunt and "stopped up" or sealed the entrances to all known setts, preventing the quarry from going to earth. Because many setts were intermittently occupied for generations, finding them was no problem. However, foxes being quick to improvise eventually would find a suitable alternate hiding place. It therefore became necessary to devise an expedient means to locate and evict foxes from the earth without resorting to extensive, time-consuming digging.

THE TERRIER'S ROLE

It seems plausible that, initially at least, any small expendable dog, game enough to pursue quarry down a hole and "draw" or bolt it back into the hunt was considered adequate. Eventually these go-to-ground dogs became known as terriers, the name derived from the Latin word *terra,* meaning earth. In all likelihood, in the early history of this canine family, "terrier" was probably a generic term for any small, rough-and-tumble dog willing to go to ground and locate foxes and other kinds of burrowing animals in their subterranean dens.

According to Dr. William Bruette's *The Complete Dog Book* (1921):

> The modern Fox Terrier was originated by Foxhound Masters, who wanted a game little sportsman of uniform size and appearance to replace the nondescript terriers which were used to bolt the fox that had gone to earth. *Before this time any dog that was plucky and whose size would permit him to go to earth was known as a Fox Terrier, no matter what his coat, color, or general appearance might be.* (Italics by author).

In time, terriers became more refined and diverse through selective breeding. Distinctive regional "types" began to evolve. Naturally, the type or variation most favored by huntsmen in any particular region of the country was the one best suited to the local game, the terrain, and prevailing hunting conditions.

From all the evidence we have, it is obvious that the history of dogs owned by British and European gentry is only one part of the terrier story. The most informative accounts of the roles that terriers played in the lives of the lower social classes are not found in Jacques de la Fouilloux's *La Venerie* (1560), Dr. John Caius' *De Canibus Brittanicis* (1570), Nicholas Cox's *The Gentleman's Recreation* (1774), William Daniel's *Rural Sports* (1801), or other early sporting classics.

Early accounts chose to ignore the importance of these dogs both to country dwellers and to "the great unwashed," wallowing in the filth and squalor of the infamous slums— the rapidly expanding industrial centers where many of the so-called "sporting terriers" seem to have originated. The reason is plain enough. All but a few peasants and laborers were illiterate. They neither wrote nor read books. But fortified with a tankard or two of hearty ale they willingly recounted their entertaining stories in rhyme and in song to all who showed an interest in their lives. This long-standing tradition preceded widespread literacy by many centuries.

Early books were penned by the learned and the aristocracy for the learned and the aristocracy. Frequently written in Latin, when such books mentioned terriers at all they focused on the sporting nature of these game little dogs, not on their origin. The history and origins of hounds and breeds favored by the socially advantaged are better documented because of the same literacy factor.

Evaluating the terriers' role in rural communities based on biased accounts written by members of the religious establishment who were often remote from the world at large is patently absurd. One of the rarest of these works is Dame Julyana Berners' (the Prioress of Sopwell) *Ye Boke of Huntying*

(15th century). A copy of this ancient work belongs to the Harvard library. The first book written in English to classify dogs was the same author's *Boke of St. Albans* (1486), in which she refers to terriers as "Teroures."

Dogs have played important roles in the lives of rich and poor alike, but in notably different ways. In *Dogs in Britain* (1948), author Clifford L. Hubbard, editor of a popular series of books called *The Dog Lover's Library*, suggests that dogs were used in drawing animals from their underground lairs for at least two hundred years. His guesstimate may have been too late by several centuries, but, on the other hand, who's counting?

Frederick W. Cousins, canine surgeon to King George V, His Royal Highness the Prince of Wales (the late Duke of Windsor), and the Kennel Club and Crufts dog shows, was a highly regarded writer of the 1930s. He was also an amazingly stereotypical, pompous, upper-class snob. In the 1934 edition of *Dogs and Their Management* (Edward Mayhew, Alfred Sewell, and Frederick Cousins—all veterinarians), a chapter devoted to hounds contains the following admonition:

> . . . woe betide the man who is caught using the word 'dog' in connection with Foxhounds. He would probably be politely asked if he were referring to 'hounds,' and still more probably the question would be put in a brusque, ironic tone which would be quite unmistakable.

A spirited account of "the hunt," dated circa 1900 (author unknown) boldly proclaimed:

> Wherever Englishmen are gathered together in possession of horses and hounds they have always hunted something. In the past their quarry included wild boar and the wolf, but now only deer and the fox are hunted in this country [the UK].

There can surely be no more moving picture than a pack of Foxhounds in full cry, all well together with their well-mounted huntsmen and whippers-in close at hand with the Master [of Hounds] and the field well spread out behind them.

As we approach the 21st century a declining number of people echo similar sentiments. Today the general public seems more concerned with the plight of the quarry than with the spectacle of the hunt or the thrill of the chase, even in Britain. Modern hounds generally follow an artificial scent laid down with a drag—usually a cloth bag permeated with game scent. Appropriately known as drag hunting, it has become a more acceptable if less traditional way to experience the thrill of riding to hounds without exploiting live foxes. Without flesh and blood foxes there is little need for hunt terriers. Consequently, our working terriers all but vanished. With the advent of Earthdog Tests, it may be time to celebrate their welcome return.

D'YE KEN JOHN PEEL?

For many socialites fox hunting was, and may remain, as much a prestigious status symbol as anything else. According to English hunting folklore, no human being ever hunted the fox with more zeal than the legendary John Peel. A fox hunting zealot of unrivaled dimension, today he would probably be regarded as a victim of an obsessive-compulsive behavior disorder.

Held in enormously high esteem by his peers, it is hardly surprising that John Peel's deeds and those of his hounds were immortalized in the most famous hunting song in the English language. The immortal words by Jack Graves were adapted to the rousing music of the ceremonial "March Past" of the Border Infantry Regiment by William Metcalf in the mid-1800s. A revised edition went on sale at Sotheby's in May 1919. In today's market the ditty would never make the charts, but as a "military two-step," in today's musical vernacular: It went number one with a bullet!

There have been countless versions of the song "John Peel," in various dialects. Most were intended to circumvent ongoing copyright disputes. The following version was probably the most popular. It needs no translation, except that "D'ye Ken?" means "do you know?":

> D'ye ken John Peel with his coat so grey?
> D'ye ken John Peel at the break o' day?

D'ye ken John Peel when he's far, far away—
With his hounds and his horn in the morning?
'Twas the sound of his horn called me from my bed,
And the cry of his hounds which he oft times led,
For Peel's view hallo would awaken the dead,
Or a fox from his lair in the morning.

Additional equally catchy verses were added over the years; enough to fill an entire book. For the sake of historical accuracy, John Peel's "coat so grey" was a faded black—a touch of poetic license there, no doubt.

A rare portrait of John Peel, the legendary fox hunter.

During World War I, "John Peel" rivaled "Dolly Grey" as the favorite morale-building song sung by troops in the trenches whenever compulsory silence was not being enforced. The following historical excerpt provides an unusual insight into the bizarre mind-set of Britain's military leaders, comprised of the social elite of barely 80 years ago:

> . . . Major-General Sir Arthur Holland once surprised a Christmas day sing-song by appearing just as "Peel's view halloo" was awakening the dead, and he expressed his delight at finding sportsmen amongst the lads.

Intended as a compliment, today one might consider the remark as a pompous, condescending assumption on the General's part, more so than a compliment. The writer goes on to recount an even more bizarre event:

> Never shall I forget a moment that burns brightly in memory's cells. It was the greatest pageantry of war sports [war sports?] France ever saw. A huge gathering of seventy thousand troops attended the sports of the Canadian Corps before they returned to the line for the final assault. *It was a lull in the sports for the observance of the high ritual of war.*
>
> The Duke of Connaught and staff, side by side with the greatest generals and commanders the war had seen, entered the ring for the massed bands and piper's pageant. The first band to swing into the enclosure was that of the 1st Canadian Division to the homely lilt of Graves' immortal inspiration "John Peel." The cheer which went up, it was discovered after, was heard in wonderment in the German trenches, not many kilometers away.
>
> If it sent a flush of pride to the brow, and a catch in the throat of any Border lad, is it to be wondered at?

No marvel either that it is called the Cumbrian National Anthem, and inspires our Northerners to noble deeds.

[Note: Cumberland lies along the southern Scottish border in the upper northwest corner of England, home to the tough and sturdy hill foxes.]

Time out! We're having a band contest over here! So much for World War I. (My grandfather left his home in Chicago and returned to Europe to fight in that war.) Let's get back on track and take a hard look at the man who became a fox hunting legend in his own time and whose deeds would be sung by Britain's schoolchildren for decades to come. Graves described Peel's four best of hounds as follows:

Ruby was the handsomest and the best. She was by a Southern sire and a clifty clean Harrier bitch. In color she was white, with a small black spot above the tail, and a little more tan on each side of the head, and partially Harrier built, but with a fine head and deep tongue, which she would give twenty yards at a breath and [Ruby] never told a lie.

Ranter was a black and tan, average tongue, about thirty-five to forty pounds in weight. Bellman was freckled with patches of black and good tan chops. Royal, like the last two hounds, was by Dancer, a half Beagle and Harrier, and had the mothers tongue.

Bellman was good but harsher.

Peel unwillingly used to say they were as good as the mother ever had [whelped], but never was there three others like them on God Almighty ground.

Ruby was kept by a dyer, and when in her prime, on a great meet, he used to dye her a sky blue to remark her feats in the field.

"Tell some of my beloved sporting countrymen, who may wish to breed hounds, how these four hounds were bred," said Peel. "They excelled equally and were equal to one another for color, figure [conformation], nose, tongue, speed and endurance."

Crack and crash Peel would fly over or through [hedgerows] on that bonny and best of bay mares, and on my soul I now believe that on such occasions he would have leapt into yawning hell and ridden over all the devils or frightened them out.

By most accounts, Peel's hounds were kept "under the greatest privation [deprivation]." Despite their renowned ability and worth, he handled them none too kindly. Apparently his peers thought no less of him for that. A fellow huntsman observed:

After a death [of a fox] he [Peel] would ruminate the hunt, and if a dog had done wrong he used to silently dismount on nearing an old very deep coal-pit and say, "Here, Shifty," The poor fond thing would come and cringe, when he would fix it [grab it] by the neck and fling it down [the coal-pit], and run away with his hand and his whip at his ears, saying, "Lard a' mercy, I could pencil him off yet."

That account does not paint a pretty picture of the man himself, but one must assume John Peel was no better or worse than other huntsmen of his day.

Because most hunts kept at least one pair of terriers, what impact, if any, John Peel and others like him had on our terrier breeds is impossible to assess. In *The Sporting Dictionary* (1803) William Taplin wrote:

With every pack of foxhounds there is seldom seen less than a brace of terriers; and, for the best reasons, one is generally larger and stronger than the other; in a small earth where one cannot enter, the other may.

Trying to handle two highly adrenalized earthdogs at the same time is no easy task for one person. Although the larger Jack Russell is stuck in the hole and needs help backing out, her impatient, smaller companion can hardly wait to take her place.

What we do know is that uncompromising attitudes like Peel's rarely change. A huntsman with little or no regard for the well-being of his hounds is unlikely to concern himself with the fate of hunt terriers. England's attitude towards animals in general was not considered harsh or brutal by foreigners. Quite the reverse in fact. In 1785, German writer J. W. Archenholtz observed:

> In England animals are treated with almost as much humanity as though they were rational beings.

What a difference a couple of centuries makes!

Glossary of Dog Terms and Colloquialisms

Action   Gait of dog, the way it walks, trots or runs.

Adrenalize   To make dogs excited and eager to perform.

Albino   A individual lacking normal pigmentation; white with pink or blue eyes.

All-rounder   A person approved by the American Kennel Club to judge all breeds of dogs at conformation shows.

American Kennel Club (AKC)   The major purebred dog registry in the United States.

Angulation   The angle at which the specific bones meet at the articulating joints: shoulder, upper arm, hip, stifle, hock.

Apple head   Rounded or dome-shaped topskull.

Apron   Long hair on the forechest; frill.

Armband   The card bearing an entry's number, worn around the handler's upper left arm while in the ring for easy identification.

AWTA   American Working Terrier Association.

Babbler   A dog that gives too much tongue (barks excessively) at the wrong time.

Back   The topline, vertebrae, or spine from withers to tail.

Bad mouth   Malocclusion; crooked or unaligned teeth; jaw over- or undershot more than the breed Standard allows.

Bait Treats or food rewards used to keep dogs alert and interested in the proceedings. To use dogs to taunt or worry wild animals for sport.

Baiting Harassing or tormenting wild animals with dogs; pitting dogs against each other or against wild animals; teasing or tantalizing a dog with food.

Balance A dog's overall appearance and degree of symmetry; correctly or incorrectly proportioned.

Bandog (obsolete) A guard dog tied up during the day and released at night.

Barrel ribs Fully sprung ribs; ribs with a circular line with approximately the same arc for the entire length of the body; barrel-shaped body, considered undesirable in most terrier breeds.

Bay To give tongue or to bark. To "hold at bay" or corner quarry.

Beard Profuse whiskers on the foreface and chin typical of most coated terriers and other broken-haired breeds.

Beefy Chunky; lacking style; overbuilt; too much dog.

Bilateral or unilateral cryptorchid A dog with one or two undescended testicles—sometimes confused with monorchidism, born with one testicle, or anorchism, born without testis.

Bitch A female canine.

Bitchy Overly refined or light-weight male; built more like a bitch than a dog; lacking substance.

Bite Placement of the upper and lower teeth when the jaws are closed: scissors bite, even bite, overshot bite, undershot bite. To attack or seize with teeth with intent to injure.

Blaze White or colored streak down center of head between eyes.

Blocky Brickhead; square formation of head or body.

Blooded Initiated; dabbed/smeared with blood from dead quarry.

Bloom Optimum coat condition (in full bloom).

Bodied up Mature; a dog with ample substance for its breed.

Bolt   To drive quarry from its den or burrow.

Bone   Skeletal development and bone density (good or bad).

Brace   Two dogs working as a pair or team; two of anything. To resist against applied pressure.

Bracemate   Either one of two dogs in a brace.

Braque   An old German term for an oversize type of Dachshund.

Brock or Grey   The Badger (Brit.).

Brindle   Irregular black or dark stripes marking a coat of lighter background, usually fawn, red or brown.

Brisket   Lower part of the forechest between the forelegs; its depth or shallowness usually judged in relation to the elbows.

Broken-coated or broken-haired   Wirehaired.

Brush   A fox's bushy tail, formerly awarded as a hunt trophy.

Burr   The formation of the inner ear.

Buttocks   The rump.

Button ear   Folded ear with short leather and the tip close to skull; e.g., Fox Terrier.

Camelback   Abnormally arched back; humpback; generally considered undesirable.

Canines   Eye teeth; fangs (two in each jaw, one located behind the incisors on each side) with which prey is seized, held or killed.

Carpals   Bones comprising the pastern joint.

Cat-foot   Tight foot; round, compact, well-arched foot.

Champion of Record (Ch.)   A dog that has satisfied the requirements for a championship and whose title has been verified and recorded by AKC or other legitimate registry.

Character   A dog's personality, disposition and demeanor, as may or may not be considered appropriate for its breed.

Cheek   Fleshy area below the eyes.

Cheeky   Round, protruding cheeks; undesirable in earthdogs.

Chest   Ribcage or torso; the forepart of the body below the shoulders.

China eye   Blue or blue-gray eye.

Chiseled   Clean-cut head, notably below the eyes.

Chops   Pendulous, fleshy jaws (uncharacteristic of terriers).

Clipping   Trimming the coat with hand-held or electric clippers (not recommended for any harsh-coated breeds).

Cloddy   Thickset; coarse.

Close behind   Moving or standing with feet and/or hocks too near each other, but not necessarily cow-hocked.

Close-coupled   Compact; short body from last rib to hip bones; short through the loins.

Coarse   Common; lacking in refinement and style; cloddy.

Cobby   Short bodied; close-coupled.

Collar   Neck restraint; ruff or white marking around neck of certain breeds.

Common   Lacking elegance; visually unappealing.

Companion Dog (CD)   official obedience title (obedience 101).

Companion Dog Excellent (CDX)   obedience award one level higher than CD.

Conformation   Physical or anatomical makeup, build or shape.

Corky   Alert, lively terrier (obsolete).

Coupling   Body length, long or short (indicated by the distance between the last rib and the hip bones).

Cow-hocked   Hocks turned inward, causing feet to turn out and producing undesirable, ungainly rear movement.

Crabbing   Sidewheeling; sidewinding.

Crated   Dogs confined to their crates while being transported, or at shows or digs.

Crest   Arch of neck; nape.

Cropped   Ears surgically trimmed to a point to make them stand erect; e.g., Manchester Terrier.

Crossing over   Or "knitting and purling"; gait erratic in front.

Croup   The rear part of the back at base of tail.

Crown   Top of the skull.

Cry   Giving tongue; baying, usually associated with scent hounds.

Culottes   Longer hair on back of thighs.

Cushion   Fullness of upper lips; e.g., Bulldog.

Cur   Old English word for "dog" that now denotes a mongrel.

Dam   Maternal parent; a bitch with puppies.

Den   The underground burrow of wild, sometimes predatory animals.

Den Dog   Earthdog; a dog sent to ground after vermin.

Den Master   The person in charge of a test site.

Dew claws   Rudimentary claws on front and/or hind legs; required in some breeds but customarily removed to avoid possible injury in the field.

Dewlap   Excess, loose skin at the throat (undesirable in terriers).

Dig (slang)   Earthdog Trial or Test.

Dish-faced   Nose higher at tip than at stop, with slight concave line between the two points.

Disqualification   An unacceptable fault or physical flaw making a dog ineligible to participate at AKC conformation events, but not necessarily in obedience or den trials; to nullify or void a win or award made at a show or trial because of a rule infraction.

Distemper teeth   Discolored and/or pitted teeth, caused by distemper or other puppy illness. An acceptable but undesirable dental condition.

Dock   To surgically shorten a dog's tail shortly after birth.

Domey   Rounded topskull.

Double coated   Weatherproof outer- and undercoat.

Down (or weak) in pastern   Loose or faulty pastern joints, suggesting lack of conditioning or poor conformation.

Down-faced   Muzzle or foreface turning downward; Roman nose; e.g., Bull Terrier.

Drag   A trail laid by dragging a heavy bag impregnated with animal scent along the ground for hounds to follow; a fake trail instead of live quarry used for pursuit in hunts.

Draw (said of a dog)   To draw or forcibly drag quarry from a den after having grabbed hold of it with its jaws; the running order.

Drive   Powerful thrusting action of the hind quarters; strong rear locomotion; also, a strong inner urge or desire.

Drop eared   Ears not erect; e.g., Norfolk Terrier.

Dry neck   Skin on throat tight; neither loose nor wrinkled.

Dudley nose   Flesh, or liver-colored nose; butterfly nose.

Dumped (slang)   Said of a dog defeated in competition.

Ear fringes   Long silky hair around the ears.

Earth   Underground den or lair of quarry.

Earthdog   A dog (or breed) built to go to ground; a dog (or breed) capable of going to ground; a den dog.

Earthdog Tests   AKC den trials.

Earthdog Titles   Junior Earthdog (JE), Senior Earthdog (SE), Master Earthdog (ME) added as a suffix to a dog's registered name.

Elbow   Joint between upper arm and forearm.

Elbowing out   Elbows turned away from the body; elbows not held close to the side of the body; loose or unsound shoulder assembly.

Entire   Males with two normal testicles descended into the scrotum.

Even or level bite   Front teeth meeting flush, with no overlapping upper or lower teeth.

Ewe-necked   Concave curvature of the neckline; weak neck.

Exhibition only   A fun run allowed at the conclusion of regular Earthdog Tests or Meets for breeds ineligible for awards.

Expression   General appearance of alertness; attitude denoting alertness and intelligence, or lack of same.

Fail   Failure to pass Earthdog Test.

Fall   Hair overhanging face; e.g., Lakeland Terrier.

Fault   An undesirable feature or characteristic that deviates significantly or otherwise from the breed standard; a mistake.

Feathering   *See* furnishings.

Fiddle face   Long, thin, snipey, pinched-in foreface.

Fill   Fullness below eyes; lack of chiseling; e.g., Bull Terrier.

Finished   A dog that has acquired an AKC championship (Ch.) title; e.g., conformation, obedience, field trail.

Flag   Long feathering on the tail of a longhaired Dachshund.

Flank   Lower body part between the last rib and the hips; the underloin.

Flat-sided (slab-sided)   Flat or straightish ribs; lacking roundness of ribs and chest; ribs not well sprung.

Flews   Pendulous lips at inner corners of the mouth.

Flicking pasterns   Extremely loose movement of the lower forelegs; faulty front movement.

Forearm   Foreleg from elbow to pastern.

Foreface   The muzzle in front of the eyes.

French front   Forelegs turned in at the pasterns and out at the elbows; forefeet at a 45-degree angle, also called fiddle or Chippendale front. A fault in most breeds.

Frill   Long hair on chest.

Fringes   Longer, often profuse hair on ears, tail, legs, belly.

Front   Forepart of body; forelegs, chest, brisket, shoulders.

Full eye   Round or prominent eye.

Fun Match or Puppy Match   Popular colloquialisms for AKC-sanctioned or unsanctioned matches—not necessarily limited to puppies.

Furnishings   The long hair on the head and legs of certain breeds.

Gait   Stride; degree of leg action when a dog is moving at its appropriate speed.

Game   Wild birds or animals originally hunted for food.

Gameness   Grit; willingness to go to ground and work quarry.

Gay tail   Tail carried above the topline.

Grizzle   Intermingling of white hairs with a colored base coat.

Groups   The seven AKC divisions into which all recognized breeds are classified.

Hackney   An abnormally high leg action in front, usually accompanied by lack of drive.

Handler   The person (professional or amateur) who actually takes a dog into the ring at a show or trial; the person who takes (handles) dogs during conformation, obedience or den trial judging.

Harefoot   Long, close-toed, narrow foot, common to certain breeds; e.g., Bedlington Terrier, Skye Terrier.

Harlequin   Large, irregular black patches on a solid white background; e.g., Great Dane.

Harsh coat   Stiff, wiry coat.

Haw   Third eyelid inside the inner corner of the eye.

Height   Measurement from the withers to ground.

High stationed   Tall; long-legged.

Hip dysplasia   One of several congenital abnormalities; a serious bone disease causing varying degrees of lameness and immobility.

Hocks   The area between the hock joint and the foot; the sole.

Hole   Colloquialism for earth or den, or den entrance.

Honor   To respect or await a bracemate's run.

Hound(s)   Dog breeds used to hunt game, used singly or in packs.

Hound ears   Long, pendulous leathers; e.g., Dachshund.

Hound marked   Tricolor; white, tan and black coat markings.

Huckle bones   Hipbones.

Hunt Terrier   A working terrier that accompanies a hunt.

Jacket   The tight body coat typical of hand-stripped, wire-coated breeds prepared for conformation shows.

Judge   The arbiter at Earthdog Tests and other competitions.

Kink tail   Bent or twisted tail.

Knee   Stifle joint; patella.

Knuckled over   A fault or condition indicating weak pasterns.

Lady pack   A pack composed of bitches, in contrast to a pack composed of all dogs.

Layback of shoulder   Angle of the scapula or shoulder blade in relation to the forearm.

Lay up   Go to ground; hide.

Leather   External ear flap.

Leggy   Too high on the leg; tall or gangly.

Level bite, pincer or even bite   Incisor teeth of upper and lower jaws meeting edge to edge. *See* Scissors bite.

Liner   The wooden frame comprising the top and two sides of man-made dens as specified by AKC and AWTA; the standard framework buried underground during the construction of a regulation tunnel for Earthdog Tests.

Loaded shoulders   Overbuilt shoulders.

Loin   Area on each side of vertebral column between last ribs and the hindquarters.

Loose leash   Dog held or led with light restraint.

Loose movement   Erratic action due to poor muscle tone or muscular development.

Low-set ears   Ears positioned or attached too low for the breed.

Low-set tail   Base of tail not a continuation of the spine; tail set below the level of topline.

Low-slung   Close to the ground; short-legged; low-stationed; e.g., Norwich Terrier.

Low-stationed   Same as low-slung.

Lower thigh   Hind leg from stifle to hock.

Lumber   Oversized; overdone; coarseness.

Lumbering   Ponderous or ungainly movement.

Lurcher   Old English for "thief"; speedy cross-bred sight hounds formerly used for poaching.

Mane   Longer hair around neck; a ruff.

Mask   Black or dark muzzle; the severed head of a fox or badger.

Muzzle   The foreface below the eye; nasal bone, nostril and jaws.

Natural earth   A den or earth made and/or used by wild quarry; a natural wild animal habitat; e.g., a badger sett.

Nose   A dog's scenting ability; e.g., has a good (or bad) nose.

Nostril   External opening of the nose.

Objection   An official protest made against an exhibitor for an alleged infraction or rule violation.

Occiput   Highest point of the backskull.

Official measurement   The height of a dog as determined and recorded by the official measuring committee at an AKC show. It is taken to determine if an exhibit conforms to the size requirements for its breed. May be requested by the judge in the ring, or by the owner prior to the commencement of judging or by a competing exhibitor during the course of judging.

OTCH   Obedience Trial Champion title prefix.

Otter head   Head resembling that of an otter; e.g., Border Terrier.

Otter tail   Tail thick at root, round and tapering.

Out at elbows   Elbows turned away from body. *See* French front.

Out at shoulder   Loose-jointed shoulder blades.

Overreaching   Gaiting fault due to a steep front and over angulated rear, causing the hind feet to overstep the front feet.

Overshot   Front teeth of upper jaw overlapping front teeth of under jaw with mouth closed; significant overbite.

Pacing   Moving both legs on one side simultaneously in the same direction; lumbering, like a bear.

Paddling   Loose, flicking motion of the forelegs, denoting weak pasterns and lack of reach.

Parti-color   Variegated in patches of two or more colors.

Pastern   Joint formed by metacarpal bones between forearm and top of foot; the wrist.

Penciling   Black lines on tan toes; e.g., Manchester Terrier.

Pigeon-toed   Toes turned inward, towards each other.

Pile   Thick, dense undercoat.

Plain   Nondescript, common.

Poach   To hunt game illegally on posted or private property.

Points   Colored markings on face, ears, legs, tail, usually white, black, or tan. Championship or title credits.

Poke   To stretch the neck forward in an abnormally low, ungainly position while gaiting.

Poor   Not in optimum condition; unthrifty; inferior.

Prick ears   Naturally erect ears; e.g., Norwich Terrier.

Pumphandle   Long tail carried high, mostly applied to hounds.

Punishing jaws   Strong, powerful jaws; a popular terrier term.

Quarry   Hunted game or vermin; e.g., foxes; entrails of game given to hounds as a reward.

Quarry at Earthdog Tests   A pair of caged laboratory rats.

Quit   To stop working quarry before the allotted time has expired.

Racy   Long-legged and lightly built.

Rangy   Similar to racy.

Rat (Rattus norvegicus)   Destructive, disease-carrying rodents, often the natural quarry of terriers.

Reach in front   The length of stride taken by the forelegs without excessive or wasted motion.

Ring steward/ judge's steward   A judge's assistant; the person responsible for marshalling and instructing trial participants in the trial area, relaying messages from the judge, etc.

Ring tail   Tail carried up and in a circle.

Ringer   A substitute with greater ability entered under the name of a lesser specimen. Absolutely banned by AKC rules.

Roach back   Convex curvature of the topline toward loin.

Roan   Fine mixture of colored hair with white hair.

Roman nose Down-faced.

Rose ear A small drop ear, folding over and back to reveal the burr.

Rudder Tail; stern—a term usually applied to hounds.

Run To go to ground; to be tested.

Running sheet (slang) Official running order or judging schedule.

Saber tail Tail carried low and curving slightly at the end.

Sable Lacing of black or dark hair in or over lighter base color.

Saddle Black marking partially covering the back.

Scapula Shoulder blade.

Scent Ground or air-borne odor emitted by animals and humans; game spoor; to lay a scent trail.

Scimitar Tail thick at the root, tapering to a fine point with the tip devoid of long hair; e.g., Bedlington Terrier.

Scissors bite Upper incisors slightly projecting beyond lowers with the inner edge just engaging the outer edge of the lowers.

Sett A natural earth or den, usually indicating that of a badger, which when abandoned is frequently taken over by foxes.

Second thigh Portion of hind leg from stifle to hock.

Self-color One color; whole color with lighter shadings.

Semi-prick ears Erect ears folded over at the tips.

Shelly Narrow chest, lacking in depth and substance.

Show dog A specimen bred more for perceived physical perfection, or fashionable appearance, than for its original function.

Sickle tail Tail carried out and up in semi-circle.

Skully Thick, coarse skull.

Slab-sided Flat-sided; flat-ribbed; little or no rib spring.

Snipey Weak, pointed muzzle; lacking underjaw.

Sorty A pack of hounds all of one sort, size and character; all alike.

Soundness   A dog's mental and physical condition.

Sparring   Allowing terriers to confront one another in the show ring to test their courage (no actual contact); favored by terrier specialists.

Spayed   Neutered; female ovaries removed surgically.

Spectacles   Shadings or dark markings over or around eyes, or from eyes to ears.

Spinner   A dog that habitually spins around in circles, thought to be suffering a brain disorder.

Square   Height at withers equal to the length from forechest to the point of rump.

Squirrel tail   Tail carried curving forward over the back.

Steward or Ring Steward   Judge's assistant in the ring.

Stifle   Joint of hind leg between thigh and second thigh.

Stilted   Choppy, uneven gait associated with steep front and rear.

Stop   Step-up from nose to skull; the indentation between eyes where nasal bone and skull meet.

Straight-hocked   Little or no angulation at hock joints; steep in rear.

Straight in pastern   Little or no bend between knee and foot.

Straight in shoulder   Minimal angulation between shoulder and upper arm.

Strip   To groom by plucking out the hair by hand or with a specialized tool. Applies to harsh-coated terriers and other breeds carrying coat types.

Subluxation   The dislocation or the displacement of certain articulating joints.

Substance   Body density; sufficient bone and muscle throughout.

Suspension   Disciplinary action banning a person and/or his dog(s) from competition.

Swayback   Sagging topline; weak back.

Thumb-marks   Black or dark spots on pasterns; e.g., Manchester Terrier.

Ticked Comparatively small areas of black or colored hair on a white or light background.

Timber Bone, especially the legs.

To get up To prepare for competition.

Topknot Covering of fine, light-colored hair on top of head; e.g., Dandie Dinmont Terrier.

Topline The back from the withers to the tail.

Trace Dark stripe down back.

Tricolor Three colors, usually white, black and tan in the same coat; e.g., Fox Terrier.

Trim To remove surplus hair in order to tidy up the coat.

Tuck-up Belly tucked in at the loins; small-waisted.

Tunnel A den; a buried den liner. A natural earth.

Typey Displaying the essential distinguishing features of a given breed; typical.

Undershot, Underbite Front teeth of the lower jaw overlapping or projecting beyond those of the upper jaw with the mouth closed (undesirable in most breeds, extremely faulty in terriers).

Upper arm The humerus; bone between shoulder and forearm.

Utility Dog (UD) Advanced obedience degree.

Utility Dog Excellent (UDX) An advanced obedience degree one level above UD.

Varminty expression The sharp, keen-eyed expression of a terrier with killer instinct.

Vent Alternative term for anus.

Vermin/Varmints Undesirable, usually destructive wild animals.

Veteran(s) Dogs seven or more years old.

Weedy Small, frail, weak; no substance.

Well let down hocks Short hocks.

Wheaten Pale yellow or fawn color.

Whiskers Long hair left on chin and muzzle of many terriers.

Wind   To catch scent of game or quarry.

Wirehaired   Hard, crisp coat; wiry-textured or broken-coated.

Withers   Point of the first dorsal vertebrae at the base of the neck—used to measure height; the highest part of a dog's body.

Wry mouth   Misaligned upper and lower jaws.

CoMMoN ABBReViATioNS

AKC   American Kennel Club
AWTA   American Working Terrier Association
B/O/H   Breeder/ Owner/ Handler
Ch.   Champion
Field Ch.   Field Trial Champion
Intro   Introduction to Quarry
JE   Junior Earthdog
ME   Master Earthdog
O/H   Owner Handler
OTCH   Obedience Trial Champion
SE   Senior Earthdog

BiBLioGRAPHY

Ash, E. *Dogs: Their History and Development*. London, 1927.

Berners, Dame J. *Ye Boke of Huntying*. London, 1486.

Bruette, W. A. *The Complete Dog Book*. Cincinnati: Stewart Kidd Co., 1921.

Caius, Dr. J. *De Canibus Brittanicus*. London, 1570.

Cheyney, E. P. *A Short History of England*. London/Boston: The Athenaeum Press, 1904.

Clarke, T. T. *The Dog Lover's Reader*. New York: Hart Publishing Co., Inc., 1977.

Cox, N. *The Gentleman's Recreation*. London, 1674.

Daniel, W. *Rural Sports*. London, 1801.

Edwards, S. *Cynographia Britannica*. Abergavenny, 1800-1805. Unfinished work published in random chapters.

Fouilloux, Jacques du. *La Venerie*, Eng. trans. Paris, 1560.

Gace de la Vigne Sur la Chasse. Paris, 1359.

Gordon, J. F. *The Bull Terrier Handbook*. 1st ed. London: Nicholson & Watson Ltd., 1957.

Hays, J., et al. *1984 Yearbook of Agriculture: Animal Health*. Washington, DC: U.S. Department of Agriculture, 1984.

Hubbard, C. L. B. *History of the Literature of British Dogs*. Ponterwyd, 1949.

LaRue, L. L., III. *Sportsman's Guide to Game Animals*. New York/London: Harper & Row, 1968.

Machucll, H. *John Peel: Famous in Sport and Song*. London: Heath Cranton Ltd., 1926.

Marvin, J. T. *The Book of All Terriers*. 2nd ed. New York: Howell Book House, Inc., 1979.

Mayhew, E. M., A. F. Sewell, and F. W. Cousens. *Dogs and Their Management*. rev. ed. London: Routledge & Kegan Paul Ltd., 1934.

Moffit, E. B. *Elias Vail Trains Gun Dogs*. New York: Orange Judd Co., Inc., 1937.

Munday, E. *The Popular Yorkshire Terrier*. London: Foyles, 1958.

Quennell, M., and C. H. B. Quennell. *The History of Everyday Things in England*. New York: Charles Scribner's Sons, 1933.

Schneider-Leyer, Dr. E. *Die Hund Der Welt*. Zurich: Albert Muller Verlag, 1960.

Smith, C. H. *Dogs*. London, 1839.

Syrotuck, W. G. *Scent and the Scenting Dog.* Rome, NY: Arner Publications, 1972.

Taplin, W. *The Sporting Dictionary.* vols. I & II. London, 1735; 1803.

Thomas, I. M. *The Welsh Terrier Handbook.* London: Nicholson & Watson Ltd., 1959.

Tuberville, G. *The Noble Art of Venerie or Hunting.* London, 1575.

Walsh, J. H. ["Stonehenge,"]. *Dog of the British Isles.* London, 1867.